B

D0181980

100 Hikes in the
GLACIER PEAK
REGION

100 Hikes in the

GLACIER PEAK REGION

**Darrington–Monte-Cristo • Glacier Peak Wilderness •
Wenatchee • Entiat**

Ira Spring and Harvey Manning
Maps by Helen Sherman

The Mountaineers
Seattle

THE MOUNTAINEERS: Organized 1906 "... to
explore, study, preserve and enjoy the
natural beauty of the Northwest."

2   1   0   9   8
7   6   5   4   3   2   1

Published by The Mountaineers, 306 Second Avenue West
Seattle, Washington 98119

Published simultaneously in Canada by Douglas & McIntyre, Ltd.
1615 Venables Street, Vancouver, British Columbia V5L 2H1

Manufactured in the United States of America

Edited by Jim Jensen
Layout by Bridget Culligan
Maps by Helen Sherman

Cover: Glacier Peak from Lake Byrne
Frontispiece: Image Lake and Glacier Peak

Library of Congress Cataloging in Publication Data

Spring, Ira.
  100 hikes in the Glacier Peak Region

  Includes Index
    1. Hiking—Washington (State)—Guide-books.
2. Hiking—Cascade Range—Guide-books.   3. Washington
(State)—Description and travel—   –Guide-
books.   4. Cascade Range—Description and travel—
Guide-books.   I. Manning, Harvey.   II. Mountaineers
(Society)   III. Title.   IV. Title: One hundred hikes
in the Glacier Peak Region.
GV199.42.W2S653   1988   917.97   88-11905
ISBN 0-89886-148-9

CONTENTS

Page

Saving Our Trails 11

Of Feet and Wheels and
Conflicts 14

Introduction 18

Location		*Page*	*Status*
Cascade River	1 Middle and South Forks Cascade River 28		North Cascades National Park and Glacier Peak Wilderness
Skagit–North Fork Stillaguamish River	2 Forgotten Trails of Finney Creek Area 30		Unprotected area
North Fork Stillaguamish River	3 Mount Higgins 32		
	4 Boulder River 34		Boulder River Wilderness
	5 Lone Tree Pass 37		
	6 Squire Creek Pass 38		
	7 Circle Peak 40		Unprotected area
	8 Huckleberry Mountain 42		
	9 Green Mountain 44		Partly in Glacier Peak Wilderness
Suiattle River	10 Bachelor Meadows 46		Glacier Peak Wilderness
	11 Milk Creek-Dolly Creek-Vista Creek Loop 49		
	12 Image Lake 50		
	13 Suiattle River to Lake Chelan 52		
	14 Around Glacier Peak 54		
Sauk River	15 Peek-A-Boo Lake 58		Unprotected area
White Chuck River	16 Meadow Mountain-Fire Mountain 60		Glacier Peak Wilderness
	17 Kennedy Ridge and Hot Springs 62		
	18 Lake Byrne 64		
	19 White Chuck Glacier 66		
North Fork Sauk River	20 Lost Creek Ridge 68		Partly in Glacier Peak Wilderness
	21 Sloan Peak Meadows 70		Henry M. Jackson Wilderness
	22 Bald Eagle Loop 72		
South Fork Sauk River	23 Stujack Pass (Mount Pugh) .. 74		Unprotected area
	24 Bedal Basin 76		Henry M. Jackson Wilderness
	25 Goat Lake 78		Partly in Henry M. Jackson Wilderness

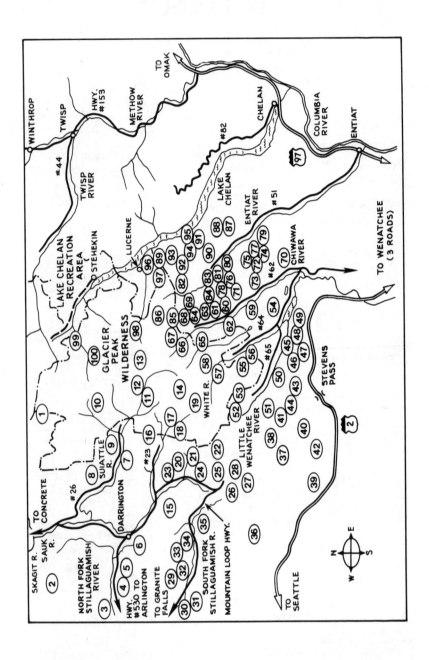

River	Trail	Page	Protection Status
South Fork Sauk River	26 Gothic Basin	80	Unprotected area
	27 Silver Lake-Twin Lakes	82	Partly in Henry M. Jackson Wilderness
	28 Glacier Basin	84	Henry M. Jackson Wilderness
South Fork Stillaguamish River	29 Goat Flats	86	Boulder River Wilderness
	30 Mount Pilchuck	89	Pilchuck State Park
	31 Bald Mountain	90	
	32 What Verlot Forgot	92	
	33 Perry Creek-Mount Forgotten	94	Unprotected area
	34 Mount Dickerman	96	
	35 Sunrise Mine Trail-Headlee Pass	98	
	36 Sultan Basin D.N.R. Trails	100	
	37 Blanca Lake	102	Partly in Henry M. Jackson Wilderness
Skykomish River	38 West Cady Ridge Loop	104	Henry M. Jackson Wilderness
	39 Barclay and Eagle Lakes	106	Unprotected area
	40 Scorpion Mountain	109	
	41 A Peach, a Pear, and a Topping	110	Henry M. Jackson Wilderness
	42 What Skykomish Forgot	112	Unprotected area
	43 Lake Valhalla	114	Partly in Henry M. Jackson Wilderness
	44 Lake Janus and Grizzly Peak	116	Henry M. Jackson Wilderness
Nason Creek	45 Nason Ridge	118	
	46 Snowy Creek-Rock Mountain	120	
	47 Rock Mountain	122	Unprotected area
	48 Merritt Lake	124	
	49 Alpine Lookout	126	
	50 Minotaur Lake	128	Henry M. Jackson Wilderness
Little Wenatchee River	51 Heather Lake	131	Partly in Henry M. Jackson Wilderness
	52 Cady Pass-Meander Meadows Loop	132	Henry M. Jackson Wilderness
	53 Poe Mountain	134	Unprotected area
	54 Dirty Face Peak	136	
White River	55 Mount David	138	
	56 Panther Creek	140	Glacier Peak Wilderness
	57 Indian Creek-White River Loop	142	

White River	58 Napeequa Valley via Boulder Pass 144	Glacier Peak Wilderness
	59 Raging Creek 146	
	60 Basalt Ridge-Garland Peak 148	Unprotected area
	61 Basalt Peak 150	
	62 Schaefer Lake 153	
	63 Rock Creek 154	Mostly unprotected area
	64 Estes Butte 156	Unprotected area
Chiwawa River	65 Napeequa Valley via Little Giant Pass 158	Glacier Peak Wilderness
	66 Buck Creek Pass-High Pass 160	
	67 Red Mountain 162	
	68 Spider Meadow 164	
	69 Carne Mountain 166	
	70 Miners Ridge 168	
	71 Alder Creek-Mad Lake 170	
	72 Mad River-Blue Creek Campground-Mad Lake 172	
	73 Hi Yu-Lost Lake Loop 175	
	74 Cougar Mountain 176	
	75 Two Little Lakes 178	Unprotected area
	76 Klone Peak Loop 180	
	77 Whistling Pig Loop 182	
	78 Entiat Mountains View 184	
	79 Tyee Ridge-Boiling Springs 186	
	80 North Tommy Ridge 188	
	81 Old Klone Peak Trail 190	
	82 Duncan Hill 192	
	83 Myrtle Lake 194	
Entiat River	84 Shetipo Creek-Devils Smokestack Loop 197	
	85 Larch Lakes Loop 200	Partly in Glacier Peak Wilderness
	86 Entiat Meadows and Ice Lakes 202	
	87 Lake Creek Basin 206	
	88 Devils Backbone 208	
	89 Big Hill-Pyramid Mountain 211	
	90 North Fork Entiat River ... 212	
North Fork Entiat River	91 Pugh Ridge 214	Unprotected area
	92 Fern Lake 216	
	93 Pyramid Mountain 218	
	94 South Pyramid Creek Loop . 220	
	95 Butte Creek-Crow Hill 222	

Lake Chelan-Stehekin River	96 Domke Lake 224	Unprotected area
	97 Emerald Park 226	Partly in Glacier Peak Wilderness
	98 Lyman Lakes 228	
	99 Agnes Creek-Lyman Lake Loops 230	Glacier Peak Wilderness
Cascade Crest	100 Pacific Crest Trail 232	

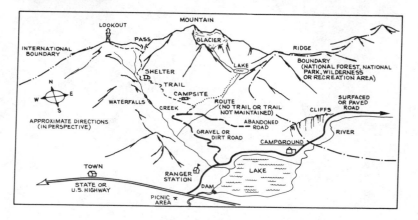

IMPORTANT NOTICE

The Forest Service has renumbered all of the forest roads in Western Washington.

The old numbering system was established more than thirty years ago, before road planners had any notion of the maze of roads that eventually would be developed. The new numbering system should make road directions easier to follow.

To avoid confusion, it is recommended that all Forest Service maps published prior to 1985, with old road numbers, be discarded and new Forest Service maps purchased at any ranger station.

Blaze on tree at Cady Pass

SAVING OUR TRAILS

Preservation Goals for the 1980s and Beyond

In the early 1960s The Mountaineers began publishing trail guides as another means of working "to preserve the natural beauty of Northwest America," through putting more feet on certain trails, in certain wildlands. We suffered no delusion that large numbers of boots improve trails or enhance wildness. However, we had learned to our rue that "you use it or lose it," that threatened areas could only be saved if they were more widely known and treasured. We were criticized in certain quarters for contributing to the deterioration of wilderness by publicizing it, and confessed the fault, but could only respond, "Which would you prefer? A hundred boots in a virgin forest? Or that many snarling wheels in a clearcut?"

As the numbers of wilderness lovers have grown so large as to endanger the qualities they love, the rules of "walking light" and "camping no trace" must be the more faithfully observed. Yet the ultimate menace to natural beauty is not hikers, no matter how destructive their boots may be, nor even how polluting their millions of *Giardia* cysts, but doomsday, arriving on two or three or four or six or eight wheels, or on tractor treads, or on whirling wings—the total conquest of the land and water and sky by machinery.

Victories Past

Conceived in campfire conversations of the 1880s, Olympic National Park was established in 1938, the grandest accomplishment of our most conservation-minded president, Franklin D. Roosevelt. (Confined to a wheelchair and never himself able to know the trails with his own feet, FDR nevertheless saw the fallacy in the sneering definition of wilderness areas as "preserves for the aristocracy of the physically fit," knew the value of dreams that never could be personally attained.)

A renewal of the campaigns after World War II brought regionally, in 1960, the Glacier Peak Wilderness and nationally, in 1964, the Wilderness Act whereby existing and future wildernesses were placed beyond the fickleness of bureaucracies, guarded by Congress and the President against thoughtless tampering.

1968 was the year of the North Cascades Act, achieving another vision of the nineteenth century, the North Cascades National Park, plus the Lake Chelan and Ross Lake National Recreation Areas, Pasayten Wilderness, and additions to the Glacier Peak Wilderness.

In 1976 the legions of citizens laboring at the grass roots, aided by the matching dedication of certain of their congressmen and senators, obtained the Alpine Lakes Wilderness.

And in 1984 the same alliance, working at the top and at the bottom and all through the middle, all across the state, won the Washington Wilderness Act encompassing more than 1,000,000 acres, including, in the purview of this volume, two new wildernesses—Boulder River and Henry M. Jackson—and additions to the Glacier Peak Wilderness.

Is, therefore, the job done?

Goals Ahead

Absolutely not.

Had hikers been content with the victory of 1938 there never would have been those of 1960, 1968, 1976, and 1984. The American nation as a whole has a step or two yet to go before attaining that condition of flawless perfection where it fits seamlessly into the final mosaic of the Infinite Plan, and the same is true of the National Wilderness Preservation System. In the trail descriptions of this book we have expressed some of the more prominent discontents with the 1984 Act.

Among the omissions are Higgins Mountain, above the Stillaguamish River; Eagle Rock, near Skykomish; and Nason Ridge, above Lake Wenatchee.

There also are faults of omission from the newly created wildernesses: from the Boulder River Wilderness, Mt. Forgotten, Mt. Dickerman, Falls Creek, and Peek-a-boo Lake; from the Henry M. Jackson Wilderness, West Cady Creek, lower Troublesome and Lake Creeks, Lake Isabel-Ragged Ridge, Gothic Basin, and Big Four Mountain.

The additions to the existing Glacier Peak Wilderness failed to include, on the west, Falls Lake-Otter Creek, Circle Peak, and the White Chuck River; and on the east, the lower Entiat River, the North Fork of the Entiat, Mad River, Schaefer and Rock Creeks.

The above is only a very partial list of the remaining tasks.

It needs to be kept uppermost in mind that designation as "wilderness" or "national park" or "national recreation area" is a means, not the end. The goals ahead are not words on a document or lines on a map but the protection of the land these symbols may signify. Any other symbols that do the job are satisfactory. The *protection* is the thing.

In contrast to the immediate past, the preservationist agenda of the immediate future (that is, the coming several years) is focused less on redrawing maps than employing any practical method to preserve roadless areas from further invasion by machinery. In fact, we are now at a stage where the saving of trails, important though that is, has a lower priority than the saving of fisheries and wildlife resources, scientific values, gene pools, and another contribution of wildland too long neglected, the provision of dependable and pure water for domestic and agricultural needs.

What in the World Happened to Us?

The wheel is more than the symbol. It is the fact. The National Wilderness Act so recognizes by banning "mechanized travel," including *but not limited to* motorized travel; bicycles—"mountain bikes"—are excluded too, for the simple reason that in appropriate terrain they readily can go 5–10 miles per hour, an "unnatural" speed often incompatible with the "natural" 1–3 miles per hour of the traveler on foot.

Outside the boundaries of dedicated wilderness, many trails can be amicably shared by bicycles and pedestrians, both capable of being quiet and minimally destructive and disruptive of the backcountry scene. Attach a motor to the wheels, however, and the route no longer deserves to be called a "trail," it becomes a *road*.

In the past quarter-century conservationists have been busy saving Washington trails by creating a new national park and a bouquet of new wildernesses. Meanwhile, the U.S. Forest Service, without benefit of environmental impact statements, has been assiduously converting *true trails* (that is, paths suitable for speeds of perhaps up to 5 or so miles per hour, the pace of a horse) to *motorcycle roads* (that is, "trails" built to let off-road vehicles—the ORV—do 15–30 miles per hour).

In this quarter-century the concerted efforts of tens of thousands of conservationists protected large expanses of wildland from invasion by machines—but during the same period a comparative handful of ORVers have taken away more miles of trails, converted them to de facto roads, than the conservationists have saved. As the score stands in 1987, only 45 percent of Washington trails are machine-free by being in national parks and wildernesses; of the other 55 percent, half are open to motorcycles—and thus are not truly trails at all.

When automobiles arrived in America the citizenry and government were quick to see they should not be permitted on sidewalks. The Forest Service (and let it be added, the Washington State Department of Natural Resources, or DNR) are slower to recognize that whenever there are more than a few scattered travelers of either kind the difference in speed and purpose between motorized wheels and muscle-powered feet is irreconcilable.

Thinking to serve the laudable purpose of supplying "a wide spectrum of recreational opportunities," the Forest Service initially tolerated ORVs, then began encouraging them, widening and straightening and smoothing "multiple-use trails" to permit higher speeds, thus increasing the number of motors and discouraging hikers, in the end creating "single-purpose ORV trails"—in a word, roads.

Federal funds were employed for the conversion until that source dried up; since 1979 the Forest Service has relied heavily on money from the State of Washington Interagency for Outdoor Recreation (IAC), the subject of the following section of this book.

Certainly, the Forest Service could not engage in such large-scale, long-term conversion of trails to roads if hikers were given the respect their numbers—overwhelming compared to the motorcyclists—deserve.

Hikers spoke up for the Washington Wilderness Act of 1984. By the many thousands they wrote letters to congressmen and senators. The pen is mightier than the wheel, and it must be taken up again, by those same tens of thousands, to write letters to congressmen and senators, with copies to the Regional Forester, Region 6, U.S.F.S., 319 S.W. Pine Street, P.O. Box 3623, Portland, Oregon 97208, asking that:

1. Trails be considered a valuable resource, treated as a separate category in all Forest Plans.
2. All trail users should be notified of public meetings concerning any Forest Plan affecting trails; public meetings should be held in metropolitan areas as well as in small, remote communities near the trails.
3. To reduce conflict between hikers and ORVs, separate motor trails need to be built, each out of sight and sound of the other.

OF FEET AND WHEELS
AND CONFLICTS

There can be 10, 100, or even 1000 hikers in a given area, and except for those actually passed on the trail, they are unaware of one another. However, the noise of even one motorcycle bounding off valley walls can disrupt the peace and quiet of hikers for miles around. Motorcyclists claim that when they drive to a nice spot they turn their motors off and enjoy the same peace and quiet that hikers do. This may be true, but it says nothing about how many people the machines disturbed before they were turned off.

On February 9, 1972, the President of the United States signed Executive Order 11644 stating "areas and trails [for ORVs] shall be located to minimize conflicts between off-road vehicle use and other existing or proposed recreational uses." Unfortunately, except where there is a serious safety problem, the Forest Service has given little consideration to the conflict between ORVs and hikers trying to get away from machines.

How do people feel about meeting other types of trail users? Because of their size, horses have "right-of-way" over motorcycles and hikers, even those hikers with heavy packs and small children, so most horse-riders don't mind other users. Because of their speed, motorcycles have "right-of-way" over hikers. Furthermore, meeting horse-riders and hikers makes cyclists think they are on a real trail and not a miniature motorcycle road, so most motorcyclists do not mind meeting other users.

To find out how hikers feel about sharing trails with motorcycles, the Washington Trails Association included at random 180 self-addressed postcards with a general mailing sent to 6000 people interested in hiking. The postcards asked five questions, and of the 180 cards mailed, 121 or 67 percent were returned, an extraordinary response.

Of the respondents, *98 percent were opposed to motorcycles on trails.* Unquestionably, the policy of encouraging motor use on multiple-use trails turns hikers away; eventually a multiple-use trail becomes a single-use road.

The conflict by no means is localized. Recreational Equipment Inc. made a national survey of its membership. Though it found only 59 percent of members were hikers, 68 percent of the total membership was opposed to motorcycles on trails. Even 28 percent of those who owned motorcycles opposed permitting them on trails.

Forest Service trails originally were built for horses to carry personnel and equipment for fire protection and were adequate for the dozen or so pack strings that used them each year. The authors remember how we hiked for days in the 1930s without meeting either horses or other hikers. In the 1950s that changed. Fire patrols switched from horses to airplanes, and trails became dominated by recreational users. The old trails in the main are still perfectly fine for hikers, but many are deteriorating with motorcycle use and the increased recreational use of horses and require rebuilding, not because of hikers but for horses and ORVs.

North wall of Baring Mountain from Eagle Lake trail

Though horses represent less than 10 percent of trail use, the Forest Service tradition of building trails for them remains evident even now. The Rattlesnake Creek trail fords the creek 14 times; two trails ford the Bumping River to reach the heart of the William O. Douglas Wilderness;

and the Snowall Creek trail in the Alpine Lakes Wilderness has two fords. By now, trail engineers with hikers in mind would have laid out different routings. Hikers, though, accepted their second-class citizenship with only a mumble. Then, suddenly, they became third-class citizens. With the advent of motorcycles came trail corners banked like a race track and 8-foot swaths cut through the forest that previously provided shade. The stepping stones a hiker yearns for were cleared from creeks to make speedy crossings for wheels.

The Forest Service estimates that hikers account for 80 percent[1] of trail use. So does 80 percent of the trail money go to hikers? I was told that *all* of the trail money goes for the benefit of hikers. Then I asked, "Just how much of the money is actually spent on hikers and how much money is used to correct problems caused by horses and machines?" Unfortunately, the Forest Service doesn't keep records that show this. Based on my 50 years of hiking, poring over Forest Service records, and talking with people, I estimated how much was spent on trails used primarily by hikers and how much was spent correcting the damage caused by horses and motorcycles on multiple-use trails. I figured that no more than one-third of all trail money was spent for the benefit of hikers, who represent 80 percent of the trail users, and that at least two-thirds of all trail money went to support horse-riders and motorcyclists.

I hope this estimate prompts the Forest Service to check its figures and tell me if I'm wrong, and if so, where. Whether I'm right or not, in so doing it will have to analyze its trail expenditures and see how little is spent enhancing the hikers' experience.

Often I ponder "multiple use." In the 1930s, when Harvey Manning and my twin brother, Bob, and I started hiking, it meant horses and hikers. Even in the 1940s and 1950s and into the 1960s, that's what it meant. Then machines began to appear on our trails, and when we questioned the Forest Service, it justified its passive acceptance of the new user by saying, "This is multiple-use." Hikers didn't speak up and the Forest Service assumed no one cared about this new addition to a growing company of backcountry travelers. If hikers had spoken, the problem never would have started, because the Forest Service would have received a resounding 98 percent[2] *"no never"* vote and found that the majority of hikers wouldn't even travel on trails that allowed motorcycles.

The Forest Service has held hearings on trail use and the ORV people made their views known and hikers didn't. With no statewide hiking organization to alert members, few hikers were even aware of the meetings. Without a real opportunity to discuss the impact on the environment with hikers or the conflict with other user groups, the Forest Service let the wheels run free on multiple-use trails and thereby encouraged a market for trail bikes that never should have been manufactured.

Some Forest Service people, serious students of the forest, recognize that machines have no place on trails. A few years ago the Twisp Ranger District closed all of its trails leading to the Chelan Summit. The ranger was overwhelmed with complaints from motorcyclists, but didn't receive a single thank-you letter from hikers, and was forced to reopen four of the trails.

Other foresters, while not absolute fans of the wheels themselves, are what they consider "reasonable" compromisers, and I've had them tell me, "Hikers and motorcyclists are just going to have to learn to live with each other" and "Hikers are selfish not to share trails." But we can't. A major reason hikers go hiking is to get away from the world that is full up with wheels. Until the middle 1960s, once on the trail, hikers were free of the noise and pollution in which we lived and worked. Now where can hikers escape? To the trails in national parks and wildernesses? Many are already so full of people fleeing from machines a person needs a permit to enter.

In the seven countries in the European Alps, all trails are closed to motorcycles. Even trails and roads used by farmers and foresters are closed to recreational use by motors. Even in Japan, where most of the machines come from, they are kept on a much tighter leash than here. Only in America. . . .

But, only in America do letters to public officials accomplish so much. There are, in the state of Washington, approximately 350,000 hikers and approximately 15,000 motorized trail-users. With such an overwhelming (20 to 1) disproportion, why do hikers have any problem? The answer is simple. The ORV industry has spent millions advertising its way to the wilderness. ORV organizations, together with individual motorcyclists and lobbyists, have been active; hikers have not. Hikers must speak for themselves, must take up their pens—their pencils—their typewriters—their word-processors—their telephones. With whatever tool, hikers must speak! Give support to hiking organizations.[3] Urge the manufacturers of your sleeping bags, tents, and packs to protect trails and join organizations that support hikers. So *speak up*. Contact the Forest Service in your favorite hiking area, write your congressman and tell him how you think trails should be managed, then send a copy of the letter to the regional forester[4]—and don't forget what happened at Twisp—compliment the Forest Service when it makes a wise decision.

Ira Spring

---

1 Estimated by the Mt. Baker—Snoqualmie National Forest. The percentage may vary from forest to forest.
2 Washington Trails Association survey, March 1984.
3 American Hiking Society, 1701 18th Street N.W., Washington, D.C. 20009, and Washington Trails Association, 16812 36th West, Lynnwood, WA 98037.
4 Regional Forester, Region 6, USFS, 319 S.W. Pine Street, P.O. Box 3623, Portland, OR 97208.

INTRODUCTION

Broad, smooth, well-marked, heavily traveled, ranger-patrolled paths safe and simple for little kids and elderly folks with no mountain training or equipment, or even for monomaniacs dashing from Canada to Mexico. Mean and cruel and mysterious routes through evil brush, over fierce rivers, up shifty screes and moraines to treacherous glaciers and appalling cliffs where none but the skilled and doughty should dare, or perhaps the deranged. Flower strolls for an afternoon, heroic adventures for a week.

A storm side (the west) where precipitation is heavy, winter long, snows deep, glaciers large, peaks sharply sculptured, vegetation lush, and high-country hiking doesn't get comfortably underway until late July. A lee side, a rainshadow side (the east) where clouds are mostly empties, summer is long, vegetation sparse, ridges round and gentle, and meadows melt free of the white by late June.

Places as thronged as a city park on Labor Day, places as lonesome as the South Pole that Scott knew. Scenes that remind of the High Sierra, scenes that remind of Alaska.

In summary, to generalize about the North Cascades: To generalize about the North Cascades is foolish.

Rules, Regulations, and Permits

Except for blocks of state (Department of Natural Resources) land around Mount Pilchuck-Sultan River and scattered enclaves of private lands mostly dating from mining and homestead days, the entirety of the Glacier Peak section of the North Cascades is federally administered. The U.S. Forest Service is the principal trustee, responsibility shared by Mt. Baker-Snoqualmie and Wenatchee National Forests.

Most of the national forest lands are under "multiple-use" administration, with roads, with logging, mining, and other economic exploitation, and with motorcycles allowed on (too) many trails. Some areas, however, have statutory protection within the National Wilderness Preservation System, where the Wilderness Act of 1964 guarantees that "the earth and its community of life are untrammeled by man, where man himself is a visitor who does not remain." The Glacier Peak Wilderness was established in 1960. The Washington Wilderness Act of 1984 made additions to this wilderness and in the Glacier Peak area of the North Cascades established new ones: the Boulder River and the Henry M. Jackson. Within these, motorized travel is banned, as is any mechanized travel, such as "mountain bikes." Horse travel is carefully regulated, and though wilderness permits have been discontinued for hikers, they are subject to restrictions on party size and camping, and must acquaint themselves with the travel regulations before setting out.

Maps

Each hike description in this book lists the appropriate topographic maps published by the U.S. Geological Survey. These can be purchased

Lyman Glacier and Upper Lyman Lake

at map stores or mountaineering equipment shops or by writing the U.S. Geological Survey, Federal Center, Denver, Colorado 80225.

The national forests publish recreation maps that are quite accurate, up-to-date, and inexpensive. Forest Service maps may be obtained at ranger stations or by writing:

Mt. Baker-Snoqualmie National Forest
1022 1st Avenue
Seattle, WA 98104

Wenatchee National Forest
P.O. Box 811
Wenatchee, WA 98801

In the national forests a traveler not only must have a map published by the Forest Service but must have a *current* map. The problem is that the Forest Service has renumbered roads, made necessary when the number of roads grew so large as to require the use of more than three digits. For instance, a spur road from road No. 12 becomes road No. 1200830, and is perhaps shown as such on the new map, though the road-side sign may be simply "830." One ranger district is using parentheses, as (1200)830; another dashes, as 1200-830; and another commas, as 1200,830.

A traveler *must* know the right numbers because in many areas the Forest Service puts no names on signs, just numbers—the new ones. Your map, if it has the old numbers, will merely deepen your confusion. And we hate to mention it, but a few of the old signs remain, with the old numbers, so that even your *new* map compounds the difficulty. A word to the wise: never leave civilization without a full tank of gas, survival rations and instructions to family or friends on when to call out the Logging Road Search and Rescue Team.

Wilmon Spires from Twin Lakes trail

Clothing and Equipment

Many trails described in this book can be walked easily and safely, at least along the lower portions, by any person capable of getting out of a car and onto his feet, and without any special equipment whatever.

To such people we can only say, "welcome to walking—but beware!" Northwest mountain weather, especially on the ocean side of the ranges, is notoriously undependable. Cloudless morning skies can be followed by afternoon deluges of rain or fierce squalls of snow. Even without a storm a person can get mighty chilly on high ridges when—as often happens—a cold wind blows under a bright sun and pure blue sky.

No one should set out on a Cascade trail, unless for a brief stroll, lacking warm long pants, wool (or the equivalent) shirt or sweater, and a windproof and rain-repellent parka, coat, or poncho. (All these in the rucksack, if not on the body during the hot hours.) And on the feet— sturdy shoes or boots plus wool socks and an extra pair of socks in the rucksack.

As for that rucksack, it should also contain the Ten Essentials, found to be so by generations of members of The Mountaineers, often from sad experience:

1. Extra clothing—more than needed in good weather.
2. Extra food—enough so something is left over at the end of the trip.
3. Sunglasses—necessary for most alpine travel and indispensable on snow.
4. Knife—for first aid and emergency firebuilding (making kindling).
5. Firestarter—a candle or chemical fuel for starting a fire with wet wood.

6. First aid kit.
7. Matches—in a waterproof container.
8. Flashlight—with extra bulb and batteries.
9. Map—be sure it's the right one for the trip.
10. Compass—be sure to know the declination, east or west.

Camping and Fires

Indiscriminate camping blights alpine meadows. A single small party may trample grass, flowers, and heather so badly they don't recover from the shock for several years. If the same spot is used several or more times a summer, year after year, the greenery vanishes, replaced by bare dirt. The respectful traveler always aims to camp in the woods, or in rocky morainal areas. These alternatives lacking, it is better to use a meadow site already bare—in technical terminology, "hardened"—rather than extend the destruction into virginal places nearby.

Particularly to be avoided are camps in soft meadows on the banks of streams and lakes (hard rock or bare-dirt or gravel sites may be quite all right). Delightful and scenic as waterside meadows are, their use may endanger the water purity, as well as the health of delicate plants. Further, no matter how "hard" the site may be, a camp on a viewpoint makes the beauty unavailable to other hikers who simply want to come and look, or eat lunch, and then go camp in the woods.

Carry a collapsible water container to minimize the trips to the water supply that beat down a path. (As a bonus, the container lets you camp high on a dry ridge, where the solitude and the views are.)

Carry a lightweight pair of camp shoes, less destructive to plants and soils than trail boots.

As the age of laissez faire camping yields to the era of thoughtful management, different policies are being adopted in different places. For example, high-use spots may be designated "Day Use Only," forbidding camps. In others there is a a blanket rule against camps within 100 feet of the water. However, in certain areas the rangers have inventoried existing camps, found 95 percent are within 100 feet of the water, and decided it is better to keep existing sites, where the vegetation long since has been gone, than to establish new "barrens" elsewhere. The rule in such places is "use established sites"; wilderness rangers on their rounds dis-establish those sites judged unacceptable.

Few shelter cabins remain—most shown on maps aren't there anymore—so always carry a tent or tarp. *Never* ditch the sleeping area unless and until essential to avoid being flooded out—and afterward be sure to fill the ditches, carefully replacing any sod that may have been dug up.

Always carry a sleeping pad of some sort to keep your bag dry and your bones comfortable. *Do not* revert to the ancient bough bed of the frontier past.

The wood fire also is nearly obsolete in the high country. At best, dry firewood is hard to find at popular camps. What's left, the picturesque silver snags and logs, is part of the scenery, too valuable to be wasted cooking a pot of soup. It should be (but isn't quite, what with the survival of little hatchets and little folks who love to wield them) needless to say that green, living wood must never be cut; it doesn't burn anyway.

Both for reasons of convenience and conservation, the highland hiker should carry a lightweight stove for cooking (or he should not cook—though the food is cold, the inner man is hot) and depend on clothing and shelter (and sunset strolls) for evening warmth. The pleasures of a roaring blaze on a cold mountain night are indisputable, but a single party on a single night may use up ingredients of the scenery that were long decades in growing, dying, and silvering.

At remote backcountry camps, and in forests, fires perhaps may still be built with a clear conscience. Again, one should minimize impact by using only established fire pits and using only dead and down wood. When finished, be certain the fire is absolutely out—drown the coals and stir them with a stick and then drown the ashes until the smoking and steaming have stopped completely and a finger stuck in the slurry feels no heat. Embers can smoulder underground in dry duff for days, spreading gradually and burning out a wide pit—or kindling trees and starting a forest fire.

If you decide to build a fire, *do not make a new fire ring*—use an existing one. In popular areas patrolled by rangers, its existence means this is an approved, "established" or "designated" campsite. If a fire ring has been heaped over with rocks, it means the site has been dis-established.

Litter and Garbage and Sanitation

Ours is a wasteful, throwaway civilization—and something is going to have to be done about that soon. Meanwhile, it is bad wildland manners to leave litter for others to worry about. The rule among considerate hikers is: *If you can carry it in full, you can carry it out empty*.

Thanks to a steady improvement in manners over recent decades, and the posting of wilderness rangers who glory in the name of garbage-collectors, American trails are cleaner than they have been since Columbus landed. Every hiker should learn to be a happy collector.

On a day hike, take back to the road (and garbage can) every last orange peel and gum wrapper.

On an overnight or longer hike, burn all paper (if a fire is built) but carry back all unburnables, including cans, metal foil, plastic, glass, and papers that won't burn.

Don't bury garbage. If fresh, animals will dig it up and scatter the remnants. Burning before burying is no answer either. Tin cans take as long as 40 years to disintegrate completely; aluminum and glass last for centuries. Further, digging pits to bury junk disturbs the ground cover, and iron eventually leaches from buried cans and "rusts" springs and creeks.

Don't leave leftover food for the next travelers; they will have their own supplies and won't be tempted by "gifts" spoiled by time or chewed by animals.

Especially don't cache plastic tarps. Weathering quickly ruins the fabric, little creatures nibble, and the result is a useless, miserable mess.

Keep the water pure. Don't wash dishes in streams or lakes, loosing food particles and detergent. Haul buckets of water off to the woods or rocks, and wash and rinse there. Eliminate body wastes in places well removed from watercourses; first dig a shallow hole in the "biological disposer layer," then, if the surroundings are absolutely non-flammable, touch a match to the toilet paper (or better, use leaves), and finally cover the evidence. So managed, the wastes are consumed in a matter of days. Where privies are provided, use them.

Water

Hikers traditionally have drunk the water in wilderness in confidence, doing their utmost to avoid contaminating it so the next person also can safely drink. But there is no assurance your predecessor has been so careful.

Goat Lake and Foggy Peak

No open water ever, nowadays, can be considered certainly safe for human consumption. Any reference in this book to "drinking water" is not a guarantee. It is entirely up to the individual to judge the situation and decide whether to take a chance.

In the late 1970s a great epidemic of giardiasis began, caused by a vicious little parasite that spends part of its life cycle swimming free in water, part in the intestinal tract of beavers and other wildlife, dogs, and people. Actually, the "epidemic" was solely in the press; *Giardia* were first identified in the 18th century and are present in the public water systems of many cities of the world and many towns in America—including some in the foothills of the Cascades. Long before the "outbreak" of "beaver fever" there was the well-known malady, the "Boy Scout trots." This is not to make light of the disease; though most humans feel no ill effects (but become carriers), others have serious symptoms which include devastating diarrhea, and the treatment is nearly as unpleasant. The reason giardiasis has become "epidemic" is that there are more people in the backcountry—more people drinking water contaminated by animals—more people contaminating the water.

Whenever in doubt, boil the water 10 minutes. Keep in mind that *Giardia* can survive in water at or near freezing for weeks or months—a snow pond is not necessarily safe. Boiling is 100 percent effective against not only *Giardia* but the myriad other filthy little blighters that may upset your digestion or—as with some forms of hepatitis—destroy your liver.

If you cannot boil, use one of the several *iodine* treatments (chlorine compounds have been found untrustworthy in wildland circumstances), such as Potable Aqua or the more complicated method that employs iodine crystals. Rumor to the contrary, iodine treatments pose no threat to the health.

Be very wary of the filters sold in backpacking shops. The technology is steadily advancing and several products already offer some protection, but as of 1987 most filters are a snare and a delusion.

Party Size

One management technique used to minimize impact in popular areas is to limit the number of people in any one group to a dozen or fewer. Hikers with very large families (or outing groups from clubs or wherever) should check the rules when planning a trip.

Pets

The handwriting is on the wall for dog owners. Pets always have been forbidden on national park trails and now some parts of wildernesses are being closed. How fast the ban spreads will depend on the owners' sensitivity, training, acceptance of responsibility, and courtesy—and on the expressed wishes of non-owners.

Where pets are permitted, even a well-behaved dog can ruin someone else's trip. Some dogs noisily defend an ill-defined territory for their master, "guard" him on the trail, snitch enemy bacon, and are quite likely to defecate on the flat bit of ground the next hiker will want to sleep on.

For a long time to come there will be plenty of "empty" country for those who hunt upland game with dogs or who simply can't enjoy a family outing without ol' Rover. However, the family that wants to go where the crowds are must leave its best friend home.

Do not depend on friendly tolerance of wilderness neighbors. Some people are so harassed at home by loose dogs that a hound in the wilderness has the same effect on them as a motorcycle. They may holler at you and turn you in to the ranger.

Dogs belong to the same family as coyotes, and even if no wildlife is visible, a dog's presence is sensed by the small wild things into whose home it is intruding.

Horses

As the backcountry population has grown, encounters between hikers and horse riders have increased. Even though hikers are unhappy when a trail has been damaged by horses or find campsites that look like barnyards, most hikers enjoy seeing the animals and accept them as part of the wilderness experience.

Most horse riders do their best to be good neighbors on the trail and know how to go about it. The typical hiker, though, is ignorant of the difficulties inherent in maneuvering a huge mass of flesh (containing a very small brain) along narrow paths on steep mountains.

The first rule is that the horse has the right of way. For his own safety as well as that of the rider, the hiker must get off the trail—on the downhill side, preferably, giving the heavy animal and its rider the inside of the tread. If necessary—as, say, on a steep hillside—retreat some distance to a safe passing point.

The second rule is that when you see the horse approaching, do not keep silent or stand still in a mistaken attempt to avoid frightening the beast. Continue normal motions and speak to it, so the creature will recognize you as just another human and not think you a silent and doubtless dangerous monster.

Finally, if you have a dog along, get a tight grip on its muzzle to stop the nipping and yapping, which may endanger the rider and, in the case of a surly horse, the dog as well.

Theft

A quarter-century ago theft from a car left at the trailhead was rare. Not now. Equipment has become so fancy and expensive, so much worth stealing, and hikers so numerous, their throngs creating large assemblages of valuables, that theft is a growing problem. Not even wilderness camps are entirely safe; a single raider hitting an unguarded camp may easily carry off several sleeping bags, a couple tents and assorted stoves, down booties, and freeze-dried strawberries—maybe $1000 worth of gear in one load! However, the professionals who do most of the stealing mainly concentrate on cars. Authorities are concerned but can't post guards at every trailhead.

Rangers have the following recommendations.

First and foremost, don't make crime profitable for the pros. If they break into a hundred cars and get nothing but moldy boots and tattered T shirts they'll give up. The best bet is to arrive in a beat-up 1960 car with doors and windows that don't close and leave in it nothing of value. If you insist on driving a nice new car, at least don't have mag wheels, tape deck, and radio, and keep it empty of gear. Don't think locks help— pros can open your car door and trunk as fast with a picklock as you can with your key. Don't imagine you can hide anything from them —they know all the hiding spots. If the hike is part of an extended car trip, arrange to store your extra equipment at a nearby motel.

Be suspicious of anyone waiting at a trailhead. One of the tricks of the trade is to sit there with a pack as if waiting for a ride, watching new arrivals unpack—and hide their valuables—and maybe even striking up a conversation to determine how long the marks will be away.

The ultimate solution, of course, is for hikers to become as poor as they were in the olden days. No criminal would consider trailheads profitable if the loot consisted solely of shabby khaki war surplus.

Safety Considerations

The reason the Ten Essentials are advised is that hiking in the backcountry entails unavoidable risk that every hiker assumes and must be aware of and respect. The fact that a trail is described in this book is not a representation that it will be safe for you. Trails vary greatly in difficulty and in the degree of conditioning and agility one needs to enjoy them safely. On some hikes routes may have changed or conditions may have deteriorated since the descriptions were written. Also, trail conditions can change even from day to day, owing to weather and other factors. A trail that is safe on a dry day or for a highly conditioned, agile, properly equipped hiker may be completely unsafe for someone else or unsafe under adverse weather conditions.

You can minimize your risks on the trail by being knowledgeable, prepared and alert. There is not space in this book for a general treatise on safety in the mountains, but there are a number of good books and public courses on the subject and you should take advantage of them to increase your knowledge. Just as important, you should always be aware of your own limitations and of conditions existing when and where you are hiking. If conditions are dangerous, or if you are not prepared to deal with them safely, choose a different hike! It's better to have a wasted drive than to be the subject of a mountain rescue.

These warnings are not intended to scare you off the trails. Hundreds of thousands of people have safe and enjoyable hikes every year. However, one element of the beauty, freedom and excitement of the wilderness is the presence of risks that do not confront us at home. When you hike you assume those risks. They can be met safely, but only if you exercise your own independent judgement and common sense.

Volunteers for Outdoor Washington

For 10,000 years or so the only trails in the North Cascades were those beaten out by the feet of deer, elk, bear, coyotes, marmots, and the folks who had trekked on over from Asia. For some 50 years, starting in the late 19th century, the "dirty miners in search of shining gold" built and maintained hundreds of miles of trails, often wide and solid enough for packtrains. During the same period many a valley had a trapline, a trapper, and a trapper's trail, and many a ridge had a sheepherder's driveway. For 30-odd years, roughly from World War I to World War II, U.S. Forest Service rangers built trails to serve fire lookouts atop peaks and to give firefighting crews quick walking to blazes. In the late 1930s the trail system attained its maximum mileage and excellence.

Then the rangers began taking to airplanes and parachutes and the miners to helicopters and the trail system began to deteriorate. Eventually the Forest Service expanded the concept of multiple-use to encompass spending money on trails where recreation was the main or only use, instead of a subsidiary one as was formerly the case. Just about that time the United States fell on hard times and the funds for Forest Service—and Park Service—trails were largely diverted to maintaining troops in foreign nations.

Volunteers for Outdoor Washington (VOW) is part of the national trend toward construction and maintenance of trails by unpaid volunteers. The principle is simple: If each hiker spends several days a year working on a crew, trails can continue to be easily walked that otherwise would be abandoned by the government for lack of money. So, would you rather devote some days to whacking at slide alder with an ax or cutting through windfall with a saw, or would you rather devote tortured hours to hauling your pack through brush and crawling over logs?

For information on how your organization, or you as an individual, can join the VOW effort, contact Volunteers for Outdoor Washington, 607 3rd Avenue, Room 210, Seattle, Washington 98104.

Protect This Land, Your Land

The Cascade country is large and rugged and wild—but it is also, and particularly in the scenic climaxes favored by hikers, a fragile country. If man is to blend into the ecosystem, rather than dominate and destroy, he must walk lightly, respectfully, always striving to make his passage through the wilderness invisible.

The public servants entrusted with administration of the region have a complex and difficult job and they desperately need the cooperation of every wildland traveler. Here, the authors would like to express appreciation to these dedicated men and women for their advice on what trips to include in this book and for their detailed review of the text and maps. Thanks are due the Superintendent of North Cascades National Park, the Supervisors of the Mt. Baker-Snoqualmie and Wenatchee National Forests, and their district rangers and other staff members.

On behalf of the U.S. Forest Service and National Park Service and The Mountaineers, we invite Americans—and all citizens of Earth—to come and see and live in some of the world's finest wildlands and to vow henceforth to share in the task of preserving the trails and ridges, lakes and rivers, forests and flower gardens for future generations, our children and grandchildren, who will need the wilderness experience at least as much as we do, and probably more.

1
MIDDLE AND SOUTH FORKS CASCADE RIVER

Round trip to South Fork trail-
  end 6 miles
Hiking time 3 hours
High point 2200 feet
Elevation gain 500 feet
Hikable June through October
One day or backpack
USGS Sonny Boy Lakes and
  Cascade Pass

Round trip to Spaulding Mine
  trail-end 7 miles
Hiking time 5 hours
High point 3200 feet
Elevation gain 1500 feet

Standing on a high summit, looking out to horizons and down to valleys, expands the spirit. Standing in a low valley, looking up from forests to summits, gives humility. To know the North Cascades a person must walk low as well as high. The Middle Fork Cascade valley is one of the "great holes" of the range, an excellent place to learn respect. The companion South Fork is one of the grandest wilderness valleys in the range, giant trees rising high—but not so high as the giant, glaciered peaks all around.

Drive Highway 20 to Marblemount and continue east 16.5 miles on the Cascade River road. Turn right on South Fork Cascade River road No. 1590, extremely rough; some people prefer to walk the 1.5 miles to the start of South Cascade River trail No. 769, elevation 1800 feet.

The first ½ mile is up and down along the river bottom to a junction. The South Fork trail goes straight ahead, crosses the Middle Fork, climbs a bit, and enters Glacier Peak Wilderness. With modest ups and downs the way proceeds through magnificent forest to the end of maintained trail at 3 miles from the road, at about 2200 feet. Good camps along the path. An extremely arduous climbers' route continues another 6 miles to Mertensia Pass, 5000 feet.

Back at the junction, the left fork, the Spaulding Mine trail No. 767 (not normally maintained and thus very brushy) climbs as steeply up along the Middle Fork as its cascades are falling down, sometimes seen

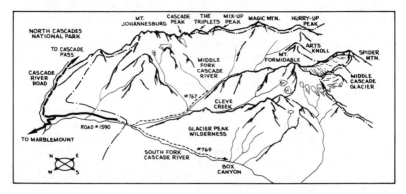

Puffball mushrooms growing beside South Cascade River trail

and always heard. At the 2400-foot lip of the hanging valley the way gentles out in a superb stand of big trees. At 2 miles is a small creek; leave the trail here and walk several hundred feet down to the riverbank for a look up avalanche-swept Cleve Creek to a glacier on the west ridge of Mt. Formidable. Back on the trail, continue upstream in sometimes forest, sometimes avalanche greenery to the trail end somewhere around 3 miles, 3200 feet. By following gravel bars of the river upstream, or gravel washes of tributary torrents up the slopes of Johannesburg, enlarged views can be obtained of the Middle Cascade Glacier, cliffs of Formidable, and the summits of Magic, Hurry-up, and Spider. Camps abound along the river.

2 FORGOTTEN TRAILS OF FINNEY CREEK AREA

Forty years ago, 100 square miles of roadless forest between Darrington and Concrete spread beneath the gaze of three fire lookouts and a lookout point, serviced by 80-odd miles of trail. Today that wildland has the look of a motheaten blanket. Clearcuts have chewed huge holes in the forest. Logging roads have obliterated 73 miles of trail. Of remaining trails, only the 4 miles to Higgins Mountain are maintained; those to the sites of vanished lookouts—Round Mountain, Finney Peak, and Gee Point—have been abandoned where not destroyed. Nevertheless, despite the moth holes, the views are still great—of the horizons, if not the near vicinity. A determined, experienced hiker equipped with a 1960s map can locate these trails.

Round Mountain

Round trip 4 miles
Hiking time 4 hours
High point 5400 feet
Elevation gain 1900 feet

Hikable July through October
One day
USGS Oso, Finney Peak

A charming Swiss-type view of mountains rising above farmlands in the Stillaguamish Valley. A trail was built here in the early 1930s but never a lookout building. Logging roads chopped the trail to a mere 2 miles and what remains has not been maintained for 30 years.

Drive Highway 530 to 5 miles west of Darrington and turn north on Swede Heaven Road (also signed 387th N.E.). Cross the river and follow road No. 18, then road No. 1850, to the unmarked trail. At first the way is an overgrown fire line, then an overgrown forest trail, and finally heather slopes.

Glacier Peak, in distance, from Round Mountain

Finney Peak

Round trip 5 miles
Hiking time 5 hours
High point 5083 feet
Elevation gain in 1200 feet, out 200
  feet

Hikable July through October
One day
USGS Oso, Finney Peak

An imposing lookout site on a rocky ridge top. In 1970 only 4½ of 15 original miles of this trail were intact. However, the Forest Service promised this remainder would be preserved. In 1975, only 2½ miles of trail survived. However, there was a promise this stretch would not be shortened and would be maintained. In 1978 only 1 mile remained and the trail was forgotten. Promises, promises. (In the near future 2½ miles of the trail may be reestablished.)

Hikers have had a tough time finding the right road in the maze of roads and the trail amongst the logging debris. Once located, the tread is still good as it follows a thin ridge crest to the lookout site.

Drive Highway 20 to Concrete, cross the river and follow South Skagit road 8 miles. Turn right on Finney-Cumberland road No. 17. At 13 miles from the highway, go left on road No. 1735 for 7.5 miles to the road-end, elevation 4000 feet.

From the road-end, if trail No. 616 can be found, climb clearcuts to the ridge top and great views. Follow the ups and downs of the crest. At 1½ miles the way enters forest, drops under cliffs, and finally switchbacks very steeply to the 5083-foot peak.

Note: the original trail along the ridge top was obliterated by logging. This may be reestablished. If it hasn't been, drive back 0.8 mile and either walk or drive road No. (1735)020 0.8 mile to its end and climb straight up the timbered hillside to intersect the original trail.

The lookout was built in 1933 and burnt in 1965. All that is left is bits of glass and rusty nails. The panoramic view is still there: saltwater shores, Olympic Mountains, Whitehorse, Glacier Peak, the Picket Range, Shuksan, Baker, and countless peaks in between.

Gee Point

Round trip 3 miles
Hiking time 2 hours
High point 4974 feet
Elevation gain about 900 feet

Hikable July through October
One day
USGS Oso, Finney Peak

The lookout once perched on this rocky summit had views up the Skagit River to Marblemount and a 360-degree panorama of mountains. This trail now receives minimal maintenance.

Drive Finney-Cumberland road No. 17 as described above, but go right on road No. 1720 and right again on road No. 1722 to the end of maintained road. Hike the abandoned ¼ mile of road to the end and find a sketchy trail climbing through a clearcut to virgin forest, where the wide tread of the original horse trail is found. In a scant mile reach the end of the horse trail at the remains of a storage shed. From here a footpath ascends, making its way up and around cliffs to the small summit at 4974 feet. The lookout cabin was built in 1930 and burnt in 1964.

Mount Higgins from trail's end

NORTH FORK STILLAGUAMISH RIVER
Unprotected area

MOUNT HIGGINS

Round trip from the trailhead 8 miles
Hiking time 6 hours
High point 4849 feet
Elevation gain 3200 feet
Hikable late June to November
One day
USGS Oso

Round trip from the switchback 6 miles
Hiking time 5 hours
Elevation gain 2500 feet

Seen from the bottom of the Stillaguamish valley, Mt. Higgins is an impressive sight, the rock strata steeply tilted, the dip slopes weathered clean enough to seem from a distance smooth enough to rollerskate or skateboard, very rapidly and finally. Seen from the top of Higgins, the horizons are equally remarkable. Located near the west edge of the Cascades, the mountain looks north, east, and south to peaks greater and icier than it is, and west to towns of the lowlands and islands in the

32

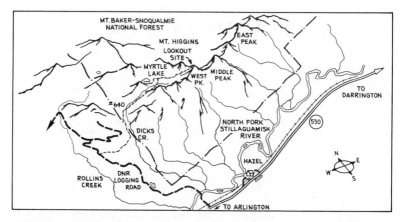

Whulj (the original residents' word for "saltwater," or "the saltwater we know"). Just a stone's throw—4500 feet—below are cornfields and pastures along the river. A person has the sensation of sitting on an overhang. This was virtually true of the fire-lookout cabin once located (and used from 1926 until 1949) atop a cliff on a 4849-foot promontory of the mountain.

Drive Highway 530 between Arlington and Darrington. Just .1 mile west of milepost 39, turn left on an unsigned, narrow, state Department of Natural Resources logging road—a poor place to be when the logging trucks are highballing. The old trail started right at the river, beginning with a ford nothing but horses ever enjoyed. This DNR road has obliterated the first 3 miles of trail; the good news, of course, is that it gets hikers across the river without risking their lives. The road is not signed. Neither are several nearby driveways. The road you want goes off the highway, crosses the railroad, and in ½ mile spans the Stillaguamish River on a concrete bridge. From there it climbs 2.9 miles to Mt. Higgins trail No. 640, elevation 1600 feet. However, any car that can drive this far probably can continue another very steep 1½ miles to a major switchback and there find a boot-beaten path which shortens the hike by 1 mile. The elevation here is about 2400 feet.

The ascent from the signed trailhead is very steep, on the order of 1200 feet a mile. The first mile has views from old clearcuts, then the way enters a deep-woods ravine. Neatly engraved on a high rock at about 2 miles is "S. Strom 8-1917," and on a corner of the rock, "K. Neste." Partly in dense forest, sometimes on rockslides, and for a bit through soggy meadow, at 3½ miles the trail reaches the lookout site and bursts out on the breathtaking view. (The summit of the mountain, 5142 feet, will attract only climbers seeking the undying glory that comes from signing a register book.)

About the names on the rock and the mountain: Walter Higgins homesteaded at Hazel, in the valley beneath the peak. Neste was an early settler-prospector. So was Sam Strom, a stubby and pugnacious Darrington Norwegian who acquired a lot of land. The Forest Service built a road on a Sauk Mountain tract Strom thought was his, so he put a gate on it and stood guard with his rifle.

4   BOULDER RIVER

Round trip 9 miles
Hiking time 3 hours
High point 1600 feet
Elevation gain 700 feet

Hikable almost all year
One day or backpack
USGS Granite Falls

See for yourself the only long, lowland, virgin-forested valley left in the Mt. Baker-Snoqualmie National Forest. The Boulder River trail once was part of the Forest Service trail over Tupso Pass and down Canyon Creek to the South Fork Stillaguamish road. It was also the shortest trail to the fire lookout on top of Three Fingers. However, when the Tupso Pass area was clearcut in the 1960s, the trail between Boulder Ford and the pass was abandoned.

The walk is especially good in late spring when the high country is still buried in snow or in late fall when the maple trees have turned yellow. There are no views of mountains, so a cloudy day is as good as a sunny one.

Drive Highway 530 east from Arlington 19.8 miles (to just beyond milepost 41) and turn right on road No. 2010 toward French Creek Campground (sign may be missing). Drive past the campground and at 3.6 miles, where the road makes a switchback, find the Boulder River trailhead, elevation 950 feet.

Trail No. 734 follows a long-abandoned railroad logging grade which ends in ¾ mile, at the edge of virgin forest. At 1¼ miles the way passes a double waterfall that plunges directly into the river—a favorite picnic spot. In ¼ mile is another lovely waterfall. With more ups than downs the trail proceeds along the valley, always in splendid forest and always within sound of the river, though it's mostly hidden in a deep canyon. At 4½ miles, 1600 feet, the trail ends abruptly at Boulder Ford. There is a campsite here and others a few feet downstream.

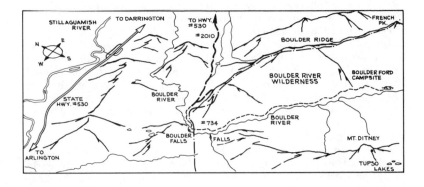

Waterfall plunging into Boulder River

Whitehorse Mountain

5̲   LONE TREE PASS

Round trip 7 miles
Hiking time 7 hours
High point 4400 feet
Elevation gain 3600 feet

Hikable July through September
One day
USGS Silverton

Built in the early 1900s by Mat Neiderprum as access to his limestone claims, this trail doesn't go anywhere near the top of Whitehorse Mountain. But it sure goes a long way up in the sky, to a little meadow with close views of a glacier and airplane-wing views to the Stillaguamish valley, where cows graze the green pastures and logging trucks rumble through the town of Darrington. Mr. Neiderprum expended minimum effort on such frivolities as switchbacks—his trail gains 3600 feet in 3½ miles. Maintenance is skimpy—some log-crawling and bushwhacking must be expected. And there is not much water. Many hikers prefer to do this in spring, going only to the first good views, turning back when snow grows deep.

Drive Highway 530 east from Arlington 24 miles. Where Swede Heaven Road goes left, turn right on Mine Road 2 miles, on pavement and then gravel, passing several houses, to the trailhead, signed "Neiderprum Trail No. 653." Elevation, 800 feet.

Though cruelly steep, the first mile of the trail is wide and smooth. In the second mile the tread is so-so (still steep). Then it becomes less a trail than a gully gouged by boots proceeding directly in the fall-line, but not always the same line; watch out for branches that dead-end. At about 3 miles additional entertainment begins to be provided by logs, mountain ash, huckleberry, salmonberry, and devils club.

At length the way enters a brushy meadow and follows a stream bed, the first and last water. At roughly 3½ miles, 4400 feet, is a tilted meadow. The alert eye can spot flats excavated for Neiderprum's cabin and toolshed. To the left is a rocky knoll, a delightful place to nurse wounds and enjoy the view down to the pastoral valley, out to peaks of the North Cascades, and up to the summit icefield of Whitehorse. Hikers stop here. Climbers, properly equipped and trained, traverse steep snow slopes to the left and cross Lone Tree Pass.

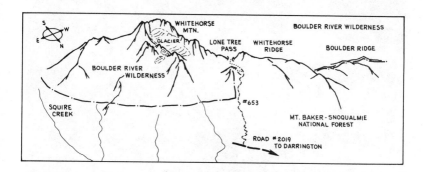

6   SQUIRE CREEK PASS

Round trip 10 miles
Hiking time 6 hours
High point 4000 feet
Elevation gain 2400 feet

Hikable July through October
One day or backpack
USGS Silverton

Hike through lovely forest to a 4000-foot pass with a dramatic view of the seldom-seen cliffs of Whitehorse, Three Fingers, and Bullon—some of the steepest and grandest walls in the western reaches of the Cascades.

From the business section of Darrington drive west 5 miles on Squire Creek road No. 2040. The road is paved in the city but quickly turns to dirt and ends in 5½ miles. The trailhead elevation is about 1600 feet.

Pick up trail No. 654. The first mile traverses a lovely valley-bottom stand of virgin forest and then the way switchbacks steeply upward on rough tread. Whitehorse and Three Fingers tantalize through the trees until approximately 3 miles, at the foot of a huge boulder field, when views open wide and grow more dramatic with each step. At 4½ miles, 4000 feet, the pass is attained. Secluded campsites are scattered about the pretty meadows, but after the snowfields melt, the water is chancy and dubious.

A shorter route to the pass—a steep 2-mile trail gaining 2200 feet misses the fine forest and has no exciting views along the way. From the business district of Darrington drive east to the edge of town, turn right, and follow the paved road up the south side of the Sauk River, the city road becoming road No. 20. In about 2 miles turn right on Clear Creek road No. 2060 about 5 miles to the trailhead, elevation 1800 feet.

Three Fingers Mountain from Squire Creek Pass trail

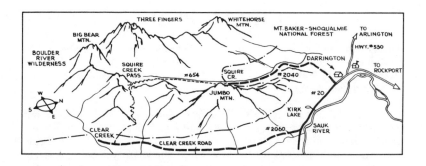

Frozen stream at Squire Creek Pass

7   CIRCLE PEAK

Round trip 4 miles
Hiking time 3 hours
High point 5983 feet
Elevation gain 2000 feet

Hikable July to November
One day
USGS Pugh Mountain

In 1967 the lookout cabin was removed and the trail abandoned, but *presently* the path *partly* survives, leading through meadow flowers, blueberries, and heather to the circle of views from Circle Peak. "Presently" and "partly" are the key words; the vicinity is being clearcut as high as chainsaws can operate without oxygen masks, 8 miles of the trail already have been obliterated, and one can only hope to convince the Forest Service to respect the value of the surviving 2 miles.

Drive road No. 530 north from Darrington or south from Rockport to near the Sauk River bridge and turn off on Suiattle River road No. 26. In 10 miles turn right on road No. 25, over the Suiattle River. In just over 3 miles more go right again on road No. 2700. At 5 miles from the river road go left on road No. 2703 for about 6½ miles to the road-end, elevation approximately 4000 feet. (When logging is completed the road will be closed; the best access then will be on another old trail, up the White Chuck River valley towards Crystal Lake.)

Circle Peak trail No. 781 may be signed. If not, climb the slope some 150 feet from the road-end and find tread. For most of the way the trail is in decent shape, a testimony to the absence of horses and motorcycles. Nature has been kind, too; surprisingly few logs must be crawled over and only in a few spots has the tread slid out. At about ⅓ mile is a stream, in the first meadow. A long ½ mile more attains the second meadow. At a long 1 mile the way switchbacks up a large meadow where the tread may be hard to find amid the hellebore, aster, bistort, valerian, and other good and bright things. At 1¾ miles the route tops a 5600-foot ridge.

A way trail switchbacks 800 feet down to Indigo Lake, in the basin

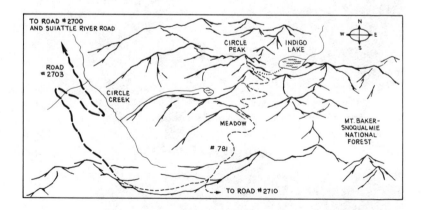

directly below. The main trail goes left, on the east slope of the ridge, climbing from a heather meadow at the end of the lookout trail, 5970 feet, to a flower-speckled rock ridge crest, 2 miles from the road. Let the eyes swing the circle of peaks—Pugh, White Chuck, Sloan, Green, Huckleberry, and, dominating all, Glacier Peak.

The lookout site isn't far away but is a rock scramble, not recommended for a hiker, and anyhow the 5983-foot summit has little more to offer.

White Chuck Mountain from Circle Mountain trail

8 HUCKLEBERRY MOUNTAIN

Round trip to viewpoint 13 miles
Hiking time 9 hours
High point 5483 feet
Elevation gain 4500 feet

Hikable July through September
One day or backpack
USGS Huckleberry Mountain

Most one-time lookout trails of the Cascades have long since had their bottoms amputated by logging trucks, and many their midsections as well, and some have been just about scalped. Clearcuts have climbed so

White Chuck Mountain from Huckleberry Mountain trail

close to timberline that hikers often pass through only the uppermost forest zones. This trail—gloryosky—has survived intact all the way from the valley to the sky. The lower stories are a virgin forest of tall, old Douglas fir and western hemlock, the middle stories are in the zones of silver fir and mountain hemlock, equally virgin, and the top stories are pristine parklands and subalpine meadows wide open to all-around views of craggy peaks and glowing glaciers. Rejoice in the bottom-to-top display of forests of the Cascade west slope. However, don't expect to pack the whole experience into a quick afternoon. Indeed, only the best-oiled hiking machines will find the trip practical for a day, and it's a long huffer-puffer with overnight packs.

Drive Suiattle River road No. 26 (Hike 7) 15 miles to Huckleberry Mountain trail No. 780, elevation 1000 feet.

The well-graded, well-maintained trail gains a steady 800 feet a mile, an ideal steepness for a hiker. The forest shadows minimize sweat and many bubbling streams are passed. At 3¾ miles is Fred Bugner Camp, about 3800 feet, with plenty of water all summer. In about 1 more mile, at about 4800 feet, is another campsite with enough water, usually—and probably the last.

At about 5 miles the grade slackens, even drops a bit, contouring below a ridge crest. Views commence, dominated by the spectacular north face of White Chuck Mountain. At 5½ miles, about 5000 feet, is a junction. The upper fork follows the wooded ridge westerly; go straight, contouring a steep slope. At 6½ miles the trail climbs into meadows, to the 5483-foot high point, and enough views to satisfy a hog. Down to the west are the logging roads of Tenas Creek; to the east, the preserved forests of Buck Creek. Across the deep valley are the emerald slopes of Green Mountain, the rocky-snowy cirques of Buckindy and Snowking, and the Pleistocene grandeur of the Glacier Peak Wilderness.

The site of the old lookout is close and the slopes to it invitingly mead-owy. To get there, however, the trail drops 400 feet from the viewpoint and then climbs 800. A party must begin thinking in terms of a 3-day or 4-day trip, backpacking a gallon of water per person to supply a dry Camp Two.

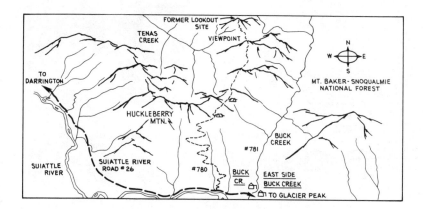

9 GREEN MOUNTAIN

Round trip 8 miles
Hiking time 6 hours
High point 6500 feet
Elevation gain 3000 feet

Hikable late June through
  October
One day or backpack
USGS Downey Mountain

The name of the peak may seem banal, but few people have ever looked up to it from the Suiattle River valley without exclaiming, "What a *green* mountain!" The trail climbs through these remarkable meadows to a lookout summit with magnificent views to every point of the compass.

Drive Suiattle River road No. 26 (Hike 7) 19 miles to Green Mountain road No. 2680. Turn left 5 miles to the road-end in a logging patch, elevation about 3500 feet. Find the trail sign above the road several hundred yards before the road-end.

The trail climbs a rather steep mile in mossy forest to a grubby hunters' camp with a year-round spring, then enters the vast meadow system admired from below. First are fields of bracken fern and subalpine plants, then, on higher switchbacks, a feast (in season) of blueberries. Views begin—down to Suiattle forests and out to White Chuck Mountain and Glacier Peak. More meadows, and views of Mt. Pugh and Sloan Peak beyond the intervening ridge of Lime Mountain.

At 2 miles, 5400 feet, the trail rounds a shoulder and in ½ mile traverses and drops 100 feet to a pair of shallow ponds amid gardens. Pleasant camps here, and all-summer water; please use established sites away from the ponds. Wood is scarce, so carry a stove.

A short way above the pond basin the trail enters a larger, wide-open basin. Please stay on the trail. The Forest Service is trying to restore the vegetation in erosion channels caused by hasty-footed hikers cutting

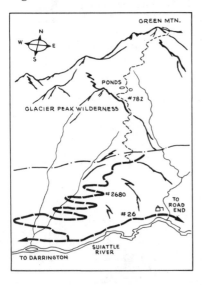

Glacier Peak from Green Mountain trail

switchbacks. The summit can now be seen directly above, and also Glacier Peak. Climb in flowers to the ridge and along the crest to the 6500-foot summit, 4 miles. A few yards below the ridge on the east is a small rocky-and-snowy basin. The delightful and scenic good-weather camps have water but no wood.

Look north along the ridge to the nearby cliffs and glaciers of 7311-foot Buckindy. Look up Downey Creek to peaks of the Ptarmigan Traverse from Dome north to Formidable. Look up Milk Creek to the Ptarmigan Glacier on Glacier Peak. Look in all directions to other peaks, too many to name.

(Left) Columbine

10   BACHELOR MEADOWS

Round trip 23½ miles
Allow 2–3 days
High point 6000 feet
Elevation gain 4600 feet

Hikable mid-July through
September
USGS Downey Mountain and
Dome Peak

A pleasant hike through virgin forest along Downey Creek to Sixmile Camp. For those with the energy and ambition, and experience in traveling rough wilderness, it's a tough climb some 5½ miles farther to meadows under 8264-foot Spire Point, with views of deep and blue Cub and Itswoot Lakes, Dome Peak, Glacier Peak, and other icy mountains.

Drive Suiattle River road No. 26 (Hike 7) 19.5 miles to Downey Creek Campground and the trailhead, elevation 1450 feet.

The first mile climbs steadily, then the way levels into easy ups and downs amid tall firs, hemlocks, and cedars, crossing small streams, sometimes coming close to the river. At 6¼ miles, 2400 feet, the trail crosses Bachelor Creek. If an overnight stop is wanted here, cross Downey to Sixmile Camp.

For Bachelor Meadows, proceed onward and now upward alongside Bachelor Creek, initially on well-graded trail and then, at 7½ miles, on a route trampled out by boots, climbing over roots and plunging through gooey bogs. The worst windfalls have been cut, but there are plenty of problems. In about 2 miles cross Bachelor Creek. The track becomes hard to follow through a boulder-strewn meadow deep in ferns and flowers. Views appear of Spire Point at the head of the valley. At about 3½ miles are a succession of good campsites; choose one under trees, away from fragile heather.

Now the trail climbs a short but steep mile and at 5400 feet abruptly leaves forest and enters an improbable little valley at a right angle to the main valley and just under Spire Point. Find water and flat campsites here in a scenic meadow.

For broader views, continue up the trail ½ mile through heather, following the small valley south to a 6000-foot pass. The trail drops ½ mile to 5338-foot Cub Lake and on down to 5015-foot Itswoot Lake.

Rather than descend, walk ¼ mile westward from the pass along a nar-

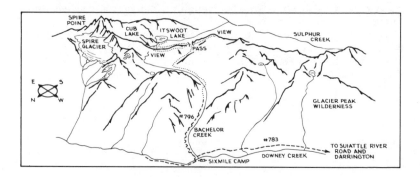

row ridge to a superb view of Dome Peak and the glistening Dome Glacier. A stone's throw below are the two lakes. South is Glacier Peak. By camping either on the ridge or at Itswoot Lake, one can explore meadow slopes eastward to a 6200-foot ridge with an even more complete view of Dome. Take pity on Cub Lake and don't camp there—its shores have been too much mangled by fishermen and climbers.

Cub Lake and Dome Peak from Bachelor Meadows trail

Glacier Peak and Milk Creek valley

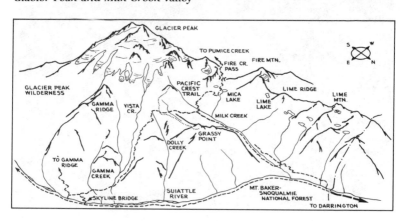

11 MILK CREEK—DOLLY CREEK— VISTA CREEK LOOP

Loop trip 33 miles
Allow 3–5 days
High point 6000 feet
Elevation gain 4400 feet

Hikable mid-July through mid-October
USGS Glacier Peak

A section of the Pacific Crest Trail climbing high on the north flanks of Glacier Peak. Massive flower fields and close-up views of the mountain. Plan to spend an extra day, at least, roaming alpine ridges.

Drive Suiattle River road No. 26 (Hike 7) 23 miles to the end, elevation 1600 feet. Walk the abandoned road 1 mile to a Y at the former road-end; take the right fork. The Milk Creek trail drops a few steps and crosses the river on a bridge. The way begins in glorious forest; at a mile or so is an awesome grove of ancient and huge cedars, hemlocks, and Douglas firs. Going sometimes level, sometimes uphill, passing cold streams, the path rounds a ridge into the valley of Milk Creek.

The trail enters a broad field of greenery at 3 miles, 2400 feet, with a stunning look up to the ice, a satisfying reward for a short trip. A pleasant campsite in the forest by the river ½ mile before the field.

From here the trail ascends gently, then steadily passes campsites in the woods, and meets the Pacific Crest Trail at 7½ miles, 3900 feet. A short bit before the junction, under an overhanging rock, is Whistle Pig Camp—a nice spot on a rainy night. (Since its former route was lost in a giant slide, the trail bypasses the site, which can, however, be reached from the top.)

Turn left at the junction and plod upward on a series of 36 switchbacks (growing views of Glacier Peak and toward Mica Lake and Fire Mountain) to the crest of Milk Creek Ridge at 11½ miles, 6000 feet. Here a climbers' route to the summit of Glacier leaves the trail, which traverses the flowery basin of the East Fork Milk Creek headwaters, crosses a ridge into the source of Dolly Creek, and at 14 miles comes to Vista Ridge and a camp, 5500 feet.

Flower gardens spread in every direction and views are grand north to Miners Ridge, Plummer Mountain, Dome Peak, and beyond. Glacier Peak is too close and foreshortened to be seen at its best. The trip schedule should include one or more walking-around days from the Vista Ridge camp. Wander up the crest to a 7000-foot knoll. Even better, hike north in meadows to 6500-foot Grassy Point, offering impressive views up and down the green valley of the Suiattle River, but especially of the white-glaciered volcano.

From the ridge the trail descends a long series of switchbacks into forest. At 20 miles, 3000 feet, is a campsite by the crossing of Vista Creek. At 21¼ miles is a junction with the Suiattle River trail and at 22 miles, 2700 feet, is a camp beside the Suiattle River. Here the trail crosses Skyline Bridge and proceeds 11 miles down the valley, reaching the road-end and completing the loop at 33 miles.

12 IMAGE LAKE

Round trip 32 miles
Allow 2–3 days
High point 6100 feet
Elevation gain 4500 feet

Hikable mid-July through
October
USGS Glacier Peak and Holden

A 2-mile-high volcano, the image of its glaciers reflected in an alpine tarn. Meadow ridges for dreamwalking. The long sweep of Suiattle River forests. Casting ballots with their feet, hikers have voted this a supreme climax of the alpine world of the North Cascades and the nation. Incredibly, Kennecott Copper Corporation still has on its long-range corporate agenda a plot to exploit a serious flaw in the Wilderness Act and dig an open-pit mine here, in the very heart of the Glacier Peak Wilderness.

Drive Suiattle River road No. 26 (Hike 7) 23 miles to the end, elevation 1600 feet. Walk abandoned roadway 1 mile to the former road-end and a Y; go left on the Suiattle River trail, largely level, partly in ancient trees, partly in young trees, sometimes with looks to the river, crossing small tributaries, to Canyon Creek Camp, 6½ miles, 2300 feet. At about 9½ miles, 2800 feet, is a creek with small campsites on both sides. Just beyond is a trail junction; go left on Miners Ridge trail No. 785. The

Sunset on Glacier Peak from Image Lake

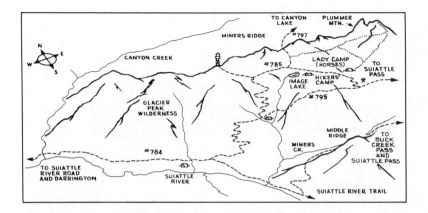

forest switchbacks are relentless and dry but with occasional glimpses, then spectacular views, out to the valley and the volcano. At 12½ miles are two welcome streams at the edge of meadow country and at 13 miles, 4800 feet, is a junction; campsites here.

Miners Cabin trail No. 795, leading to Suiattle Pass, goes straight ahead from the junction; take the left fork to Image Lake. Switchback up and up, into blueberry and flower meadows to expanding views, to a junction atop Miners Ridge, about 15 miles, 6150 feet. A ¼-mile trail leads to Miners Ridge Lookout, 6210 feet. The main trail goes right ¾ mile, traversing, then dropping a bit, to 6050-foot Image Lake.

Solitude is not the name of the game here. Indeed, so dense is the summer population that the Forest Service, to protect fragile meadows, has prohibited camping around and above the lake; it further has banned swimming when the water is low, to keep the water pure. Below the lake ¼ mile is a hikers' camp. A mile away at Lady Camp are accommodations for horses and mice. (On a bench above the trail look for the lovely lady carved in a tree by a sheepherder in about 1916.)

Exploring the basin, climbing the 6758-foot knoll above, visiting the fire lookout, walking the Canyon Lake trail into the headwaters of Canyon Creek—thus one may fill memorable days. By no means omit the finest wandering of all, along the wide crest of Miners Ridge, through flower gardens, looking north to Dome Peak and south across Suiattle forests to Glacier Peak. Experienced scramblers can ascend steep heather to the 7870-foot summit of Plummer Mountain and wide horizons of wild peaks.

Also, hike the grassy trail east 1 mile to lovely Lady Camp Basin. Here is the west edge of the ½-mile-wide open-pit mine Kennecott wants to dig; this blasphemy has been prevented so far by violent objections from citizen-hikers but can only be stopped for good and all by your letters to congressmen and senators urging them to exercise the right of eminent domain and purchase the patented mining claims. From Lady Camp the trail drops some 500 feet in ½ mile to a junction with the Suiattle Pass trail, which can be followed 1¾ miles back to the Image Lake trail junction.

Lyman Lake

SUIATTLE RIVER
Glacier Peak Wilderness

13 SUIATTLE RIVER TO LAKE CHELAN

One-way trip 29½ miles
Allow 5–7 days
High point 6438 feet
Elevation gain about 5000 feet

Hikable mid-July through
September
USGS Glacier Peak, Holden,
Lucerne

A rich, extended sampler of the Glacier Peak Wilderness, beginning in green-mossy westside trees, rising to flowers of Miners Ridge and views of Glacier Peak, crossing Suiattle and Cloudy Passes, descending parklands of Lyman Lake to rainshadow forests of Railroad Creek and Lake Chelan. The traverse can be done in either direction; the west-to-east route is described here.

Drive to the Suiattle River road-end, 1600 feet, and hike 11 miles on the Suiattle River trail to the 4800-foot junction with the Image Lake trail (Hike 12).

Continue straight ahead on Miners Cabin trail, climbing 1¾ miles to a second junction with the Image Lake trail, 5500 feet. (The lake can— and should, if time allows—be included in the trip by taking the lake trail, which is 4½ miles long from end to end, thus adding some 3 extra miles and about 600 feet of extra elevation gained and lost.) In trees just past the junction are miners' shacks belonging to Kennecott Copper and a spring, a bad-weather campsite. The way now contours, crossing one huge and many small avalanche paths, entering open slopes with grand views to Fortress, Chiwawa, and other peaks at the head of Miners Creek, passing more miners' junk in a small flat, and at 17 miles reaches Suiattle Pass, 5983 feet. A bit before the pass and below the trail is a pleasant camp on a meadow bench.

The trail drops some 300 feet into headwaters of South Fork Agnes Creek (when the snow is gone the drop can be partially avoided by taking a rough hiker-only alternate path) and climbs to the most spectacular views and gardens of the trip at 6438-foot Cloudy Pass, 19 miles. (From here, easy meadows demand a sidetrip to 7915-foot Cloudy Peak and along the ridge toward 8068-foot North Star Mountain.)

Descend magnificent flowers, then subalpine forest, to 5587-foot Lyman Lake, 21 miles. There are campsites in the woods north of the lake and at the outlet, but camps above, under Cloudy Peak, have better views and fewer bugs. If a campfire is built, use an existing fire ring. From the lake outlet, a hiker-only trail climbs 500 feet to Upper Lyman Lake (Hike 98). At the lake begin bear problems which continue the full length of the Railroad Creek valley; look to the defense of your good things.

The trail drops past the outlet creek of Lyman Lake, where frothy water pours down long, clean granite slabs, and switchbacks into forests of Railroad Creek; views of Crown Point Falls and Hart Lake. After boggy walking and several bridges, at 24½ miles, 3989 feet, is Rebel Camp and at 25½ miles is Hart Lake. Both have good camping.

The last portion of the route is over blocks of rock under a tall cliff, past tumbling waterfalls, occasional views of high peaks, to beaver bottom and green jungle, and finally a jeep track and baseball field to the abandoned mining town of Holden, 29½ miles, 3200 feet.

Holden Village Inc. uses the old town as a religious retreat but may sell a hiker ice cream. A road goes 12 miles down to Lucerne, on Lake Chelan, a hot and dusty walk, or hike trail No. 1240 past Domke Lake to Lucerne (Hike 96). From May 15 to October 15 (check with the Forest Service-Park Service Information Center in Seattle) a bus from Lucerne Resort makes four daily round trips, permitting hikers to catch the *Lady of the Lake* downlake to Chelan (Hike 96) and a bus home.

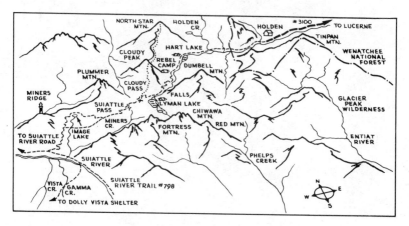

14 AROUND GLACIER PEAK

One-way trip (north and east
  section) 52 miles
Allow 5 days minimum
High point 6409 feet (Little Giant
  Pass)
Elevation gain 9800 feet
To: Buck Creek Pass 4100 feet
  Little Giant Pass 3800 feet
  Boulder Pass 1550 feet
Hikable late July through
  September
USGS Glacier Peak and Holden

One-way trip (south and west
  section) 43 miles
Allow 5 days minimum
High point 6450 feet (Red Pass)
Elevation gain 5700 feet
To: White Pass 3700 feet
  Red Pass 700 feet
  Fire Creek Pass 2000 feet

    Mt. Rainier National Park has the Wonderland Trail; the Glacier Peak Wilderness offers an equally classic and less crowded around-the-mountain hike. The 96-mile circuit with an estimated 15,500 feet of climbing includes virgin forests, glacial streams, alpine meadows, and ever-changing views of the "last wild volcano."

    The complete trip requires a minimum 10 days, and this makes no allowance for explorations and bad-weather layovers. However, the loop breaks logically into two sections which can be taken separately. Perhaps the ideal schedule is to do the entire circuit on a single 2-week jaunt, keeping packs to a reasonable weight by arranging to be met midway with additional supplies.

Indian Head Peak from White Pass

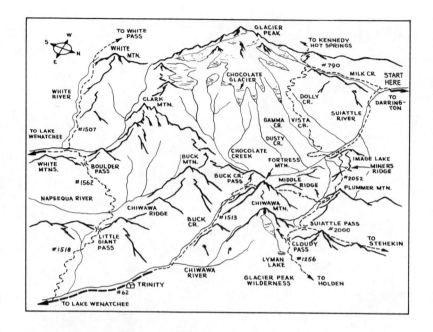

North and East Section

Begin at Suiattle River road-end (Hike 13). Hike 11 miles along the Suiattle River on trail No. 784 to a junction with the Pacific Crest Trail. Go right 4½ miles to Middle Ridge trail and climb 5 miles to Buck Creek Pass.

(Two partial alternate routes can be taken; each adds a day and many extra rewards. One is the Milk Creek—Dolly—Vista Creek trail (Hike 11), which starts at Suiattle River road-end and rejoins the main route near the 10-mile marker; this alternate adds 12 miles and 3200 feet of elevation gain to the total. The other is the Image Lake—Miners Ridge trail (Hike 12), which leaves the main route at 9½ miles and rejoins it 6 miles below Buck Creek Pass; this alternate adds 8 miles and 1700 feet of elevation gain. The two alternates can be combined on a single trip; first do the Milk Creek—Dolly—Vista trail, then backtrack 1 mile to begin the Image Lake—Miners Ridge trail.)

Descend 9½ miles from Buck Creek Pass to Trinity (Hike 66) and walk 5½ miles down the Chiwawa River road to Little Giant trail No. 1518. Climb 4¾ miles to Little Giant Pass (Hike 65) and descend 1¾ miles into the Napeequa River valley and a junction with Boulder Pass trail No. 1562. Climb 6½ miles over the pass and down to the White River trail (Hike 58). If the trip is to be broken at this point, hike 3½ miles down-river to the White River road.

A possible itinerary (excluding the alternates) would be: Day One, 11 miles and a 1150-foot climb to Miners Creek (the best camping is on the river ¼ mile beyond Miners Creek); Day Two, 9½ miles and a 3200-foot climb to Buck Creek Pass; Day Three, descend 3350 feet in 15 miles to

Ptarmigan in summer plumage

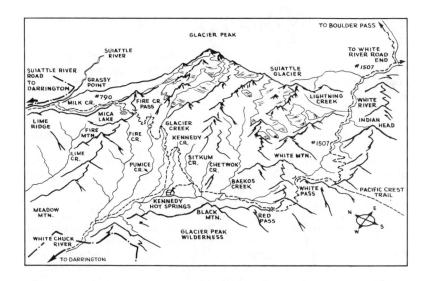

Maple Creek; Day Four, climb 3900 feet, descend 2300 feet, in the 6½ miles to Napeequa River; Day Five, 10 miles to White River road-end, a climb of 1550 feet and a descent of 3350 feet. However, frequent campsites along the route allow shorter days or different days.

South and West Section

Begin at White River road-end. Hike 14¼ miles on White River trail No. 1507 to an intersection with the Pacific Crest Trail. Continue north on the crest 2 miles to White Pass (Hike 55).

From White Pass contour and climb to Red Pass in 2 miles, then descend the White Chuck River (Hike 19) 7 miles to a junction. For the main route, climb right on the Pacific Crest Trail, crossing headwaters of Kennedy Creek, Glacier Creek, Pumice Creek, and Fire Creek and reaching Fire Creek Pass in 8 miles (Hike 17).

(For an inviting alternate, go 1½ miles from the junction downriver to Kennedy Hot Springs, enjoy a hot bath, then continue a short ½ mile to the Kennedy Ridge trail (Hike 17) and climb to rejoin the main route; this alternate adds 1¼ miles and 800 feet of elevation gain to the total.)

From Fire Creek Pass, the snowiest part of the entire circuit, descend a valley of moraines and ponds, past the magnificent cold cirque of Mica Lake, reaching the Dolly-Vista trail junction in 4 miles. Continue 7½ miles down Milk Creek trail to the Suiattle River road-end (Hike 11).

A possible itinerary would be: Day One, 9 miles and climb 800 feet to Lightning Creek; Day Two, 9¼ miles, a gain of 2100 feet and a loss of 1000 feet, to Glacier Peak Meadows; Day Three, drop 1700 feet and climb 2250 on the 9½ miles to Pumice Creek; Day Four, 500 feet up and 900 feet down on 4¼ miles to Mica Lake; Day Five, 11 miles and 3800 feet down to Suiattle River road. Again, frequent campsites allow shorter or different days.

15   PEEK-A-BOO LAKE

Round trip 7 miles
Hiking time 4 hours
High point 4300 feet
Elevation gain 1400 feet in, 400
   feet out

Hikable July through October
One day or backpack
USGS White Chuck Mountain

A forest trail climbs to a delightful meadow with a spectacular view, then drops to a lake set in the deep woods of a deep cirque.

Drive from Darrington on the Mountain Loop Highway, road No. 20, along the west side of the Sauk River to just short of the Sauk River bridge. Turn right on road No. 2080 for 1.1 miles and turn right again on road No. 2081, signed "Peek-A-Boo Lake 4 miles." At 2.8 miles from the highway keep right and at 3.1 miles go left on road No. 2084. A word of caution: Road No. 2084 is drivable but at survey time alder trees had crowded in from the sides. They leave a passageway barely wide enough for a skinny car to squeeze through the remaining 1.5 miles to what was originally a wide parking area and turnaround. It now is so overgrown there is room for only three or four cars. Park here, elevation 2800 feet. The road goes on but soon deteriorates to a jeep track.

Peek-A-Boo Lake Trail No. 656 climbs steeply along the jeep track ⅓ mile to where even jeeps quit and the road narrows to a footpath. Note the stumps with springboard notches from logging operations in the late 1940s. At approximately 1 mile the road ends and the trail enters virgin forest.

Relentless switchbacks ascend to a 4300-foot high point from which easy ups and downs lead to a small pond and a pretty meadow. For the trip climax, leave the trail and cross the meadow to the spectacular viewpoint. See White Chuck Mountain and Mt. Pugh. Look down better than half a vertical mile to the Sauk River and out to the White Chuck River.

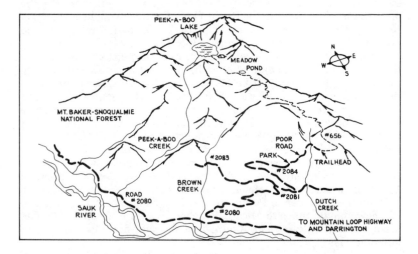

The glacier-white summit of Dome Peak stands above Meadow Ridge, and Mt. Shuksan rises in the distance.

From the meadow the trail deteriorates to a boot-beaten path as it descends 400 feet to the lakeshore and campsites.

Peek-A-Boo Lake

16 MEADOW MOUNTAIN— FIRE MOUNTAIN

Round trip to 5800-foot viewpoint
  18 miles
Allow 2 days
High point 5800 feet
Elevation gain 3500 feet
Hikable July through October
USGS Pugh Mountain and Glacier
  Peak

One-way trip to White Chuck
  River road-end 21 miles
Allow 2–4 days
High point 5800 feet
Elevation gain 4600 feet

Meadows laced with alpine trees, views to White Chuck forests and Glacier Peak ice, and a long parkland ridge for roaming, with sidetrips to cirque lakes. But be warned: there is a 5-mile road walk to the trailhead with little protection from the sun. Some of the misery is compensated for by spectacular views of Mt. Pugh and Glacier Peak.

Drive from Darrington on the Mountain Loop Highway 10.5 miles. A short distance beyond the Sauk River bridge is a major junction. Go left on White Chuck River road No. 23 for 5.5 miles, then left on the Straight Creek road No. 27 signed "Rat Trap Pass," for another 2 miles and park at the beginning of Meadow Mountain road No. 2710, elevation 2350 feet.

Glacier Peak from Meadow Mountain

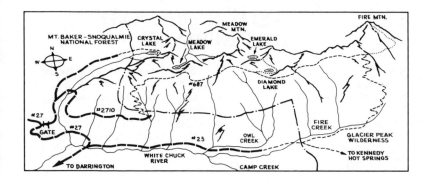

Walk road No. 2710 5 miles, passing Crystal Creek at 2 miles, to the road-end and trailhead at 3400 feet.

The trail climbs a steep 1¼ miles (but in deep, cool forest) to the first meadow. Cross a bubbling brook in an open basin and then choose either of two destinations, both offering splendid views down to the green valley and out to the peaks. For the easiest, follow a faint way trail 1 mile westward to a high knoll, about 5600 feet. For the best, and with the most flowers, hike the main trail 2 miles eastward, climbing to a 5800-foot spur ridge from Meadow Mountain.

For one of the great backpacking ridge walks in the Glacier Peak Wilderness, take the up-and-down trail traversing the ridge east toward Fire Mountain. Earlier camps are possible, but the first site with guaranteed all-summer water is Owl Creek at 7 miles, ½ mile beyond the 5800-foot viewpoint, in a bouldery basin to which the trail drops to avoid cliffs of Meadow Mountain.

Going up, then down, then up again, at 10¼ miles the trail touches the 5850-foot ridge crest. From here, descend 1 mile northwest on a much-used but not-obvious and easily lost path to 5300-foot Diamond Lake. From the east side of the lake climb a wide gully up the low ridge and descend extremely steep slopes (no trail) to Emerald Lake, 5200 feet. Good camps at both; stay 100 feet from the shores.

The main trail continues along the ridge to a low saddle at about 9 miles. The path proceeds east through patches of trees, grassy swales, sidehill flowers, and views.

At 10½ miles is a magnificent camp in a cliff-walled basin and at 12 miles, beneath Fire Mountain, are charming garden camps near the site of long-gone Fire Chief Shelter. From this area experienced off-trail travelers can find an easy but not obvious route to the summit of 6591-foot Fire Mountain; if the terrain gets steep and scary, you're on the wrong route—turn back.

The trail descends an old burn to Fire Creek forests, joining the White Chuck trail at 16½ miles, 1½ miles from the White Chuck River road. By use of two cars, one parked at each road-end, hikers can enjoy a 20-mile one-way trip along the full length of the ridge trail; a 3-day schedule allows for sidetrips, but more days could easily be spent exploring.

17   KENNEDY RIDGE AND HOT SPRINGS

Round trip to Kennedy Hot Springs 11 miles	Round trip to Kennedy Ridge moraine 18 miles
Hiking time 5 hours	Hiking time 8–10 hours
High point 3300 feet	High point 6200 feet
Elevation gain 1000 feet	Elevation gain 4000 feet
Hikable May through November	Hikable July through October
One day or backpack	
USGS Glacier Peak	

Two hikes which can be done separately or combined. A short-and-low trip leads through tall, old trees, beside a roaring river, to volcano-warmed waters—the most mob-jammed spot in the Glacier Peak Wilderness. A long-and-high trip climbs to alpine flowers with a close look at icefalls tumbling from Glacier Peak.

Drive White Chuck River road No. 23 (Hike 16) 10 miles to the road-end parking area and campground, elevation 2300 feet.

The wide, gentle White Chuck River trail has become—deservedly—the most popular valley walk in the Glacier Peak area. The way goes through virgin forest always near and sometimes beside the ice-fed river, beneath striking cliffs of volcanic tuff, crossing the frothing tributaries of Fire, Pumice, and Glacier Creeks. At 5 miles, 3300 feet, is a junction with the Kennedy Ridge trail.

Kennedy Hot Springs: In 1976 a flood ravaged the White Chuck River trail to Kennedy Creek. The trail has been restored to the guard station, hot springs, and camp, 3300 feet. The beautiful forest is the proper reward of hiking to Kennedy, but an amazing percentage of the 6000 people who annually sign the register come for the hot (actually, only warm) springs. To satisfy geological curiosity, cross the river on a bridge, turn left, and in a few yards come to the cruddy, rusty waters

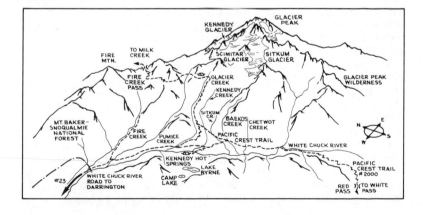

Glacier Peak from Kennedy Ridge

seeping from the earth. A tublike pool has been dug, just big enough for three or four people who don't believe in the germ theory of disease.

The waiting line gets long at the pool in good weather. It would be a lot shorter if folks knew that in summer the coliform bacteria count exceeds that of the average sewer.

Kennedy Ridge: From the junction at 5 miles, just before crossing Kennedy Creek, climb left on the Kennedy Ridge trail. (A full canteen is needed.) The steep forest way, with occasional glimpses of ice, joins the Pacific Crest Trail at 2 miles, 4150 feet. The Crest Trail switchbacks through cliffs of red and gray andesite, then along heather parklands on a moraine crest, swinging left to reach the welcome splash (and camp-site) of Glacier Creek at 5650 feet, 4 miles from the White Chuck River trail.

Leave the trail and climb open subalpine forests on the old moraine, then in ½ mile step suddenly out onto raw boulders of a much newer moraine. See the Kennedy and Scimitar Glaciers tumbling down the volcano.

It's a shame to turn back at the edge of so much good highland roaming. Just 1 mile from Glacier Creek, over Glacier Ridge, are the splendid meadows and camps of Pumice Creek, and in 3½ miles more is Fire Creek Pass.

Lake Byrne

WHITE CHUCK RIVER
Glacier Peak Wilderness

LAKE BYRNE

Round trip 16 miles
Allow 2–3 days
High point 5500 feet
Elevation gain 3200 feet

Hikable August through
    September
USGS Glacier Peak and Pugh
    Mountain

In olden times, when it took 2 full days of hiking up the White Chuck River just to get to Kennedy Hot Springs, pedestrians never devoted less than a week to the trip. The glorious forest was savored fully. The springs were much enjoyed after sessions of trail-sweating, and with rel-

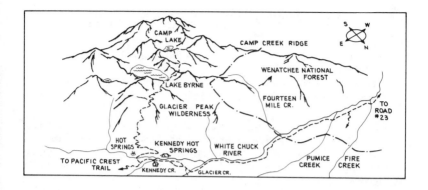

ative safety, the bathers being few and their diseases not terribly fearsome. However, the cherry on the tip of the whipped cream was Lake Byrne and the highland roaming westward from there. For modern weekenders, however, backpacking to the lake is something of a horror story. The last chapter—the trail from hot springs to lake—is short, but *steep*. And spots near the lake where a sleeping bag can be spread are so few that some campers pitch tents on the lake itself, which is usually frozen solid all but a few weeks of late summer. No fires permitted, of course. The recommendation, therefore, is to basecamp at Kennedy and day-hike to the lake and the meadow ridges above.

Drive White Chuck River road No. 23 (Hike 16) 10 miles to the road-end parking area and campground, elevation 2300 feet.

Hike 5½ miles to the patrol cabin at Kennedy Hot Springs (Hike 17) and find a campsite on either side of the White Chuck River, 3300 feet.

From the patrol cabin cross the footbridge to a junction. The left fork goes 100 yards to the warm (80–90 degrees) springs, which you will not wish to put your own body in but which may contain bodies worth looking at. The right fork climbs a bit, past campsites, and then takes dead aim on the sky, gaining 2200 feet in the next 2½ miles. The good news is that horses try it so rarely that the tread is well preserved.

The first 1¼ miles from the hot springs are well shaded, with glimpses through chinks in the green wall of the blinding snows of Glacier Peak. A fairly level and quite brief respite from steepness has heather meadows, a small stream, and possible camping. Then, upward again, the views get bigger and the trail poorer. At 2½ miles from the hot springs, 8 miles from the road, is Lake Byrne, 5500 feet.

The shores are mostly steep heather meadows, rockslides, cliffs, and snowfields. The few campsites are widely scattered around parkland knolls; if you arrive late on a busy weekend, inspect your chosen spot to see whether campers on the other side of the knoll have been using it for other purposes.

For meadows that grow wider and views that expand constantly, take the right fork at the lakeshore and climb 500 feet more to a viewpoint overlooking Camp Lake, set in a deep, cold little bowl where the sun rarely shines and the snow hardly ever melts.

19 WHITE CHUCK GLACIER

Round trip 28 miles
Allow 4 days minimum
High point about 6500 feet
Elevation gain 4200 feet

Hikable late July through
September
USGS Glacier Peak

Begin beside a loud river in deep forest. Walk miles through big trees; climb to little trees and wide meadows. Roam flowers and waterfalls and moraines to a broad glacier. Wander gardens and ridges. In the opinion of some experts, this is the supreme low-to-high tour of the Glacier Peak Wilderness.

Drive to the White Chuck River road-end, 2300 feet, and hike 5½ miles to 3300-foot Kennedy Hot Springs (Hike 17).

Ascend steeply then gently to join the Pacific Crest Trail at Sitkum Creek, 3850 feet, 7 miles from the road; camping space is available here when Kennedy is full-up, as it often is. The Crest Trail continues along the valley, passing the avalanche track and meadow-marsh of Chetwot Creek, fording Baekos Creek, and at 9½ miles, 4000 feet, crossing a high bridge over the rocky chasm and thundering falls of the White Chuck River.

Now the trail climbs a valley step. Trees are smaller and so is the river, assembling itself from snow-fed tributaries. A little meadow gives promise of what lies above. After more subalpine forest, the way enters the tremendous open basin of Glacier Peak Meadows. At 12 miles, 5400 feet, is the site of the long-gone Glacier Peak Shelter, with magnificent campsites everywhere around.

As a base for easy hiker-type explorations, this highland valley of flowers and creeks and snowfields is unsurpassed in the North Cascades.

First off, if your hike is mid-August or later, visit the ice; before that it is covered with snow. Climb meadows around the valley corner east, taking any of many appealing routes to a chilly flatland of moss and meanders, to moraines and meltwater, and finally the White Chuck Glacier. The white plateau is tempting, but only climbers with rope and ice ax should venture on its surface.

For another trip, investigate the intriguing White Chuck Cinder Cone, the remnant of a volcano smaller and newer than Glacier Peak. Scramble meadows higher to the 6999-foot summit of Portal Peak.

If your visit is in late July or early August it is flower time on White Mountain. Therefore, hike the Crest Trail 2 miles up a wintry, rocky basin to 6450-foot Red Pass; from here, continue on the trail to White Pass (in early July be careful of the steep snow slopes) or leave the trail in about ½ mile and follow the flower crest to the summit of 7030-foot White Mountain.

Every direction calls. Invent your own wanderings. The minimum trip to the glacier can be done in 3 days but any itinerary of less than a week will leave the visitor frustrated, determined to return soon to finish the job at leisure.

Campsites other than those mentioned above are plentiful along the trail and throughout the high basin. However, as a conservation rule to be followed here and everywhere, camps should be placed in trees adjacent to meadows, not in the actual meadows, which are so fragile that only a few nights of camping can destroy nature's work of decades.

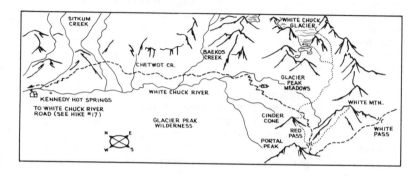

Glacier Peak from White Mountain

20 LOST CREEK RIDGE

**Round trip to Round Lake
  viewpoint 10 miles
Hiking time 6–8 hours
High point 5550 feet
Elevation gain 3550 feet
Hikable July through October
One day or backpack
USGS Sloan Peak**

**Round trip to Lake Byrne 24 miles
Allow 3 days minimum
High point 6000 feet
Elevation gain about 6500 feet
Hikable August through October
USGS Glacier Peak and Sloan
  Peak**

A long ridge of green meadows, alpine lakes, and wide views of peaks near and far—one of the most memorable highland trails in the Glacier Peak region. The ridge can be ascended from either end for day trips or overnight camps, or walked the full length on an extended backpack. However, the middle section of the route is a boot-beaten path, often overgrown. Particularly in the fog, hikers must be careful not to get lost on Lost Ridge.

Drive from Darrington on the Mountain Loop Highway 17 miles to

Sloan Peak from Lost Creek Ridge trail

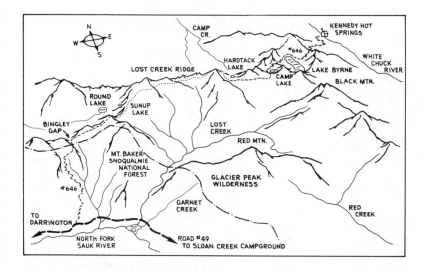

North Fork Sauk River road No. 49. Turn left 3 miles to a small parking area and trail sign, elevation 2000 feet.

The trail goes gently along the valley ½ mile, then climbs steeply through open woods, with occasional views of impressive Sloan Peak, to 4425-foot Bingley Gap, 3 miles. The way continues some 2 miles up and along the ridge to meadows and a 5550-foot saddle overlooking Round Lake, 5100 feet. (A steep sidetrail descends to the lake and good camps.) Scramble up the grassy knoll east of the saddle for more views of Sloan and a look at Glacier Peak. Here is the place for day-trippers to have lunch, soak up the scenery, and return home; generally the trail is reasonably snowfree by early July.

Beyond this point is a stretch of route with no real trail. The practice used to be to build trail through patches of woods but leave travelers to find their own way across meadows. Routefinding is easiest when the snow is mostly gone, by late July. Though upsydownsy, the going is easy and glorious—always near or on the crest, mostly past vast meadows, through open basins, near small lakes, with constant and changing views, and a choice of delightful camps. Near Hardtack Lake continuous tread begins. At 11 miles, the trail now good, is 5650-foot Camp Lake, set in a cliff-walled cirque; near the lake is a gully that is extremely dangerous when full of snow. The trail climbs to a 6000-foot knob, drops a few feet to the rocky basin of "Little Siberia," then descends to famous Lake Byrne, 12 miles, 5550 feet. Flowers and rocks and waterfalls of the basin and adjoining ridges demand leisurely exploration, ever dominated by the tall white volcano rising beyond White Chuck River forests. However, campsites at Lake Byrne are so small, poor, and overused that exploration should be basecamped at Camp Lake or Kennedy Hot Springs.

From the lake the trail abruptly drops 2250 feet in 2 miles to Kennedy Hot Springs (Hike 17). If transportation can be arranged, such as by use of two cars, a 19-mile one-way trip can be done; allow 3 days or more.

21 SLOAN PEAK MEADOWS

Round trip 8 miles
Hiking time 7 hours
High point 4800 feet
Elevation gain 2900 feet

Hikable mid-July through
 September
One day or backpack
USGS Sloan Peak

The big-time, big-corporation prospectors of today racket about the sky in fleets of helicopters and never touch the ground except to drill holes in it and heap garbage on it. Their predecessors of 50 to 100 years ago, earthbound "dirty miners in search of shining gold," spent half their time building trails—often steep, but wide and solid enough for pack-trains. Hundreds of miles of trails still in use were engineered by these old-timers, who never found gold or anything else of value, earned nothing for their sweat but a shirt that needed a bath.

One bit of their handiwork, the Cougar Creek trail, climbs from the North Fork Sauk River to meadows on the side of Sloan Peak. This would be a glorious spot to spend a couple of days roaming, but lacking dirty miners to maintain it, the trail has become so mean that hauling camping gear to the high country would try the cheerfulness of a Sherpa. Even as a day trip it's no simple stroll. Crossing the North Fork Sauk and Cougar Creek is always difficult and frequently impossible. If in doubt, return to the car and go someplace else, such as Lost Creek Ridge (Hike 20).

Drive from Darrington 17 miles on the Mountain Loop Highway to North Fork Sauk River road No. 49 and turn left 4.6 miles to the trail-head, signed "Climbers' Trail," elevation 1900 feet.

Walk ½ mile to the river on abandoned road, in several places flooded by beaver ponds. The bridge is decades gone and unless a logjam can be found upstream or down the trip is over—the river is much too deep and swift to ford safely.

On the far side of the river the trail follows an old logging railroad grade ¼ mile, then gains 500 feet up an old clearcut to the old miners' trail. Steep but wide, the relic ascends a long 2 miles to a rotten-log (obviously not permanent) crossing of Cougar Creek between two water-

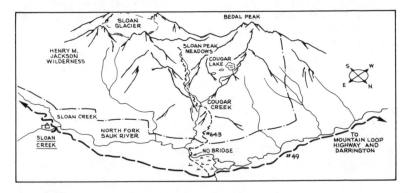

Cougar Creek

falls. In the next 2 miles the creek is crossed twice more—or perhaps not
at all on a hot day when meltwater is roaring. The way continues relentlessly up, crossing four more creeks, each at the base of a waterfall.
(Waterfalls are among the best parts of this hike.)

At a very long 4 miles, elevation 4800 feet, a small meadow invites
camping, in views up to Sloan Glacier and the summit cliffs of Sloan
Peak and out east to Red Mountain and Glacier Peak. The slopes above
the camp meadow invite wandering—which, however, should go only to
the first steep snowfield unless the party has climbing gear and skills.

Monte Cristo peaks from Bald Eagle Mountain trail

NORTH FORK SAUK RIVER
Henry M. Jackson Wilderness

22   BALD EAGLE LOOP

**One-way trip 24 miles plus 2½ mile
   walk on road
Allow 3 days
High point 6000 feet
Elevation gain 4500 feet**

**Hikable late July through
   September
USGS Blanca Lake, Benchmark
   Mountain, Glacier Peak, Sloan
   Peak**

A ramble through miles of alpine trees and meadows on lonesome trails used more by deer and marmots than people, which is surprising considering the beauty. The trip must be planned with care to end each day at a place with camping space—and water, which is scarce on the high ridges. After a spot at 1 mile on the abandoned road, the next for-sure water is at Spring Camp, 9 miles. However, in early summer there normally are snowbanks that can be cooked in a pot.

Drive from Darrington 17 miles on the Mountain Loop Highway and turn left on North Fork Sauk River road No. 49. In 7 miles, pass Sloan Creek Campground, the end of the loop trip. Drive another 2 miles to a junction with an unnumbered road and turn right on it a few hundred feet to Sloan Creek and a washed-out bridge, the present (1987) Bald Eagle Mountain trailhead, elevation 2400 feet, the start of the loop trip. A good plan is to unload packs here and park the car back near the campground, where you'll be coming out.

Walk 2½ miles on abandoned logging road to the end and find the start of trail No. 1050, elevation 3200 feet. The way traverses a clearcut, enters forest, and climbs a sometimes muddy 1½ miles to Curry Gap, 4000 feet, and a junction. Go left on Bald Eagle trail No. 650, climbing nearly to the top of 5668-foot Bald Eagle Mountain. With ups and downs, pass Long John Camp (often dry) at 8 miles from the washed-out bridge and Spring Camp at 9 miles. The trail then climbs within a few yards of the crest of 5946-foot June Mountain. Be sure to take the short sidetrip to the summit for views of Sloan Peak, Monte Cristo peaks, Glacier Peak, valleys, and forest. The tread on the north side of June Mountain may be covered by steep, hard snow. If so, climb above—with care, since the heather also is steep and slippery.

At 12½ miles is a junction. The trail to the right continues 3 miles to Dishpan Gap and the Pacific Crest Trail. Go left on trail No. 652, dropping 500 feet, and at 14 miles reach 5500-foot Upper Blue Lake, usually frozen until mid-August; the best camps are near the upper lake.

From Upper Blue Lake the trail climbs 500 feet onto Pilot Ridge for 5 miles of some of the finest ridge-walking in the North Cascades. Finally the trail leaves the ridge and drops 3000 feet in an endless series of short, steep switchbacks to North Fork Sauk River trail No. 649, at 11½ miles from Upper Blue Lake reaching Sloan Creek Campground, 24 miles from the start. If you adopted the good plan your car awaits you here, rather than 2½ miles away at the washed-out bridge.

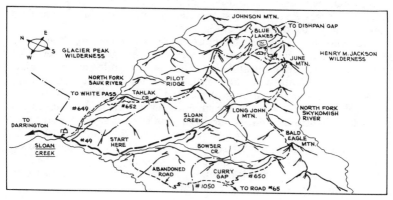

23 STUJACK PASS (MOUNT PUGH)

Round trip to Stujack Pass 7½ miles
Hiking time 6–7 hours
High point 5500 feet
Elevation gain 3600 feet
Hikable mid-July through October
One day or backpack
USGS Pugh Mountain and White Chuck Mountain

Round trip to Mt. Pugh 10 miles
Hiking time 10–12 hours
High point 7201 feet
Elevation gain 5300 feet
Hikable August through October

A strikingly high and imposing peak, considering its position so far west from the main mountain mass; the height and the detachment make for an exceptional viewpoint. See out to lowlands of the Whulj (the original residents' name for "the saltwater"). See the North Cascades from Baker to Eldorado to Dome to Bonanza. See nearby Glacier Peak standing magnificently tall above White Chuck River forests. Closer, see the superb horn of Sloan and the sharp peaks of the Monte Cristo area. A rare panorama indeed, but not for everyone—the upper portion of the trail once led to a fire lookout but has long been abandoned and now is climbers' terrain. However, hikers can go most of the way and see most of the horizons.

Drive from Darrington on the Mountain Loop Highway 14 miles to Mt. Pugh road No. 2095. Turn left 1 mile to Mt. Pugh trail sign, elevation 1900 feet.

The steep trail climbs cool forest 1½ miles to tiny Lake Metan, 3180 feet, and the first outward looks. Just before the lake are springs providing the last dependable all-summer water. Relentless switchbacks ascend to meadows, 3 miles, beyond which point the trail is not maintained. The only decent camps on the route are here, but water may be gone by late summer.

Three Fingers and Whitehorse appear beyond valley forests as the trail switchbacks up talus and flowers to the notch of Stujack Pass, 3¾ miles, 5500 feet. Inexperienced travelers should have lunch and turn back, content with a full bag of scenery.

Those who go beyond Stujack must be trained and equipped for steep snow travel (early summer) and for rock scrambling (all summer). The abandoned trail climbs abruptly from the pass to a knife-edge rock ridge, then picks a delicate way along cliffs above a glacier trough, perhaps vanishing occasionally in snowfields. Part of the trail was dynamited from rock to provide access to the summit lookout; the first cabin was destroyed by lightning, and its successor was burned several years ago. Steep heather and rock slabs lead to the summit, 5½ miles, 7201 feet.

The summit views are worth the effort for travelers who can use ice ax, hands and feet, and perhaps rope, and thus manage the upper "trail" in safety. The views short of the summit are also worthwhile; be sure to stop, satisfied, when the going gets scary.

White Chuck Mountain from Stujack Pass

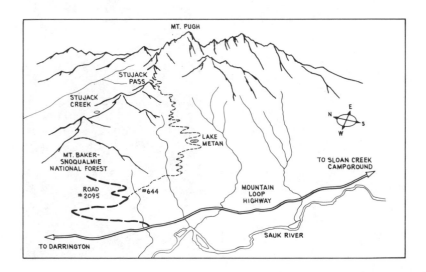

SOUTH FORK SAUK RIVER
Henry M. Jackson Wilderness

24   BEDAL BASIN

Round trip 6 miles
Hiking time 6 hours
High point 5000 feet
Elevation gain 2200 feet

Hikable July through October
One day or backpack
USGS Sloan Peak and Bedal

Lovely and lonesome alpine meadows beneath the towering south wall of Sloan Peak. The long-abandoned miners' trail is rough and sketchy, recommended only for experienced hikers who don't mind sweating for the sake of solitude.

Drive from Darrington 18 miles, .8 mile beyond the North Fork Sauk River bridge. Turn left on road No. 4096 for 2 miles to trail No. 705 (unsigned), elevation about 2800 feet. If you reach Bedal Creek, you've driven ¼ mile too far.

The trail gains altitude steadily, alternating between cool forest and sun-hot avalanche tracks choked with ferns, salmonberry bushes, and a spicing of nettles. Occasionally the Forest Service sends a brushing crew up the lower trail, which thus is better walking some years than others. If a crew hasn't been along recently, be prepared to foot-probe blindly for the tread in shoulder-high greenery.

At 1½ miles, amid big trees beside the creek, is a campsite much-used by Sloan climbers of years past, before another summit approach became more popular. Cross Bedal Creek here—hopefully on a log. The way gentles out in a broad avalanche area of alder and vine maple and a gathering of tributaries. At 2 miles recross the creek.

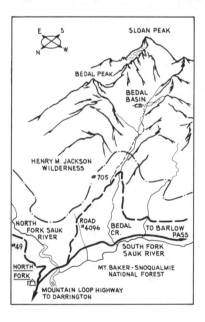

The trail becomes obscure (unless the Forest Service unexpectedly takes up the job started by Harry Bedal many decades ago). The route is steep, ascending an abrupt valley step. Faint tread gains a few hundred feet along the left side of the creek, now quite small, crosses to the right side, and—probably—vanishes. If so, continue upward several hundred feet, cross the creek to the left side, and climb open timber. When the left side gets brushy, cross to forest on the right side and ascend huckleberry slopes to a collapsed mine with a stream flowing from the mouth. About 100 feet higher, rediscover the faint trail, which contours right, into open meadows at the lip of the basin, 5000 feet.

Above is the wall of Sloan. Monster boulders fringe the heather-and-flower floor of the basin. Near a great block of rock on the right side of the meadow are rotten logs of Harry Bedal's cabin, which along about 1940 succumbed to the crushing winter snows. Splendid camps all around. From the pass at the basin head are broad views.

(Opposite) Clark's nutcracker (Above) Harry Bedal's cabin

GOAT LAKE

Round trip 10 miles
Hiking time 5 hours
High point 3162 feet
Elevation gain 1280 feet

Hikable mid-June through
 October
One day or backpack
USGS Sloan Peak and Bedal

A subalpine lake beneath cliffs and glaciers, a popular destination with hikers of all ages. Wander beside clear, cold water, investigate artifacts of long-ago mining, and admire snow-fed waterfalls frothing down rock walls. The trail (foot travel only) partly traces the route of a wagon road dating from the late 19th century.

Drive from Verlot on the Mountain Loop Highway, crossing over Barlow Pass and descending into the South Fork Sauk River valley. At approximately 23.5 miles, turn right on Elliott Creek road No. 4080 and drive 1 mile to the trailhead parking lot, elevation 1900 feet.

Once the trail was within sight of Elliott Creek but heavy hiker use has turned swampy areas into huge impassable quagmires. Until expensive repairs can be made, trail No. 647 follows an abandoned logging road shaded by young alder trees. At 3½ miles the road ends and the way drops a bit to follow the all-but-vanished route of a wagon road that once reached the mining settlement and hotel near Goat Lake.

At approximately 4 miles from the parking area the trail enters the Henry M. Jackson Wilderness. At 4½ miles the trail leaves the wagon road, steepens, and switchbacks upward, reaching the outlet of Goat Lake at 5 miles, elevation 3162 feet.

For an interesting sidetrip, at about the 4-mile mark the wagon route diverges rightward from the trail and crosses Elliott Creek to decrepit remains of a mining settlement. The wagon route then switchbacks and in roughly ½ mile recrosses the creek on risky remnants of a bridge to meet the trail.

Enjoy the views of Foggy Peak. Prowl relics of what was, some 75 years ago, a busy mining town. In summer sunshine, take a brisk swim.

Beyond the outlet is a nice spot to picnic. The trail continues left

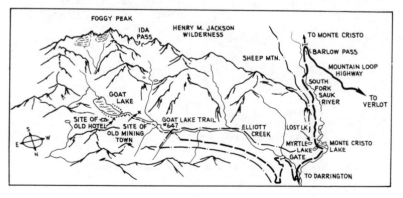

around the shore, eventually disappearing in alder and vine maple. On a rocky knoll before the brush begins is a particularly fine place to sit and stare and eat lunch before going home.

Because campers have overused the lakeshore areas, these are now restricted to picnicking. Camping is permitted only at the old hotel site on a knoll above the outlet. Fires are prohibited.

Goat Lake

26 GOTHIC BASIN

Round trip from Barlow Pass 9 miles
Hiking time 9 hours
High point 5000 feet
Elevation gain 2600 feet

Hikable late July through early October
One day or backpack
USGS Monte Cristo

A glacier-gouged basin designed for wandering. Rounded buttresses polished and scratched by ice, sparkling ponds in scooped-out rock, an Arctic-barren cirque lake, loud waterfalls, meadow nooks, old mines, ore samples, and views of Monte Cristo peaks.

From 1909 to 1912 the Northwest Mining Company operated a 7,000-foot aerial tram from Weden House to a mine just below the basin lip. Little evidence is left except a few bits of rusty iron, some rotten wood, and the trail. For years after the railroad fell into disuse the headwaters of the South Fork Sauk reverted to wildness. Then, in the 1940s, the American dream of getting everywhere by car produced a road to Monte Cristo. As a day-after-Christmas present to pedestrians, in 1980 the Sauk River washed out long stretches of the road. (In the destruction of silly roads is the preservation of wilderness.)

Gothic Basin

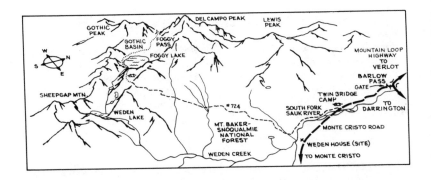

Drive 19.5 miles from the Verlot Public Service Center to Barlow Pass and park near the gated Monte Cristo road, elevation 2360 feet.

Walk the Monte Cristo road 1 mile to the crossing of the Sauk River and just before crossing find a new trailhead on the right-hand side, behind an outhouse, elevation 2400 feet. The miners' trail started from Weden House, ¼ mile farther, but keeping a bridge over the braided channels was nigh impossible. In 1983, therefore, members of Volunteers for Outdoor Washington (VOW), led by Will Thompson, roughed out a path ½ mile along the riverbank to intersect the old trail.

Note: The VOW shortcut trail, though not posh, is easily walkable; by *not* crossing the river it gives safe access in the highest of water. The "official trail" (signed "Weden Creek," which is not where the trail goes) requires a river crossing which is rarely simple and often very dangerous.

The sturdy miners didn't waste effort on switchbacks and the trail is steep all the way. At 1½ miles is a series of three streams rushing down slot gorges possibly snow-filled and dangerous until early August; here too are flowers, a mine, and views across Weden Creek to Silvertip Peak. The trail enters brush, the tread gets skimpy and requires some careful walking, and the grade continues grueling. "King Kong's Showerbath" demands a halt amid unpleasantness for refreshment. The Consolidated Mine invites a sidetrip. After an especially straight-up and rock-scrambling stretch, the way emerges into a final ½ mile of heather and flowers, traversing the valley wall on meadow shelves.

At 3 miles, 5000 feet, the trail cuts through the ridge into Gothic Basin and ends in a meadow among buttresses. There is a good campsite here and many others throughout the basin. Wood is scarce; bring a stove.

Now, explorations. In the lower basin are flower gardens, artifacts of old-time (and as recent as 1969) prospecting, waterfall gorges, and views down to Weden Creek and across to the Monte Cristo group. Especially fascinating are the rocks: limestone, sandstone, conglomerate, granite, and iron-red mineralized zones, all plucked and polished by the ice, the dominant brownish limestone weathered into oddly beautiful forms. Follow the streambed or the buttress crest 300 feet higher to Foggy (Crater) Lake, in a solemn cirque under Gothic and Del Campo Peaks. Scramble slabs and talus and blossoms to 5500-foot Foggy Pass between Gothic and Del Campo for higher views.

27 SILVER LAKE-TWIN LAKES

**Round trip from Barlow Pass to
    Silver Lake 11 miles
Hiking time 8 hours
High point 4350 feet
Elevation gain 3000 feet
Hikable July through October
Backpack
USGS Monte Cristo**

**Round trip to Twin Lakes 17 miles
Hiking time 12 hours
High point 5400 feet
Elevation gain 3500 feet in, 1000
    feet out**

Three beautiful lakes, especially lovely in fall colors. The nearest and easiest, Silver Lake, is tucked in a cirque of cliffs, waterfalls, and meadows. Twin Lakes, 3 grueling miles farther, are twin pools of deep blue beneath the great east face of Columbia Peak.

The authors don't want to hear any hikers whimpering about the December 26, 1980, flood that ripped up the road to Monte Cristo and forced them to walk 4 extra miles, each way. The Christmas flood was the best thing that's happened to this valley since the railroad shut down. The 4 miles now free of automobiles are the most scenic valley walk, forest walk, river walk in the area, with many excellent backpacker campsites, a terrific place to introduce little children to a life away from automobiles. Further, those 4 miles multiplied by 2 convert certain former day walks amid crowds to lonesome wildland backpacks. If you phone the Verlot Service Center (206-691-7791) for the latest road information, and they say it's still closed, break into a cheer and write a letter to the Snohomish County Council telling them to keep it that way.

Drive the Mountain Loop Highway 19.5 miles from the Verlot Public Service Center to Barlow Pass and park near the gated Monte Cristo road, elevation 2360 feet.

Hike the Monte Cristo road 4 delightful miles to a junction. The left is to Glacier Basin. Take the right toward Monte Cristo townsite, cross the

Silver Tip Peak and Twin Lakes trail

Sauk River, and in a few feet reach the trailhead, elevation 2753 feet, signed "Silver Lake."

The trail is steep, eroded by water and boots, and cluttered by boulders, giant roots, and stumps from clearcutting on private property, so though it's only 1½ miles to Silver Lake, expect to spend 2 hours getting there. At 4350 feet the way crosses Poodle Dog Pass. Here the Silver Lake and the Twin Lakes trails separate.

For Silver Lake, go right from the pass ¼ mile to the shore, 4260 feet. Camping is possible by the outlet but the space is cramped and muddy. No fires permitted; bring a stove. For the best views and picnics cross the outlet and climb open slopes 700 feet to a shoulder of Silvertip Peak. Look down Silver Creek toward Mineral City and beyond Silver Lake to the Monte Cristo peaks. In season, graze blue fruit.

For Twin Lakes, go left on a boot-beaten track that follows an old miners' trail. The way is strenuous and rugged, gaining (and partly losing) 1500 feet in the 2½ miles to a viewpoint 650 feet above the lakes. Though the route is well defined it would be easy to lose in snow, so don't go before August. In the first mile the up-down trail rounds a ridge with views out Silver Creek to logging roads. After dropping to pass under a cliff, at about 2 miles it climbs to a viewpoint over the deep hole of Seventysix Gulch to Wilmon Spires.

Walk on—and scramble along, above cliffs—the ridge crest. Some 150 feet before the highest point of the ridge the trail contours right toward an obvious pass, and at 2½ miles reaches the lakes view, far enough for most hikers. Make a wrong turn here and you're in cliffs. To reach the lakes go right, descending to the obvious pass and then following the trail down a wide terrace. Campsites are plentiful, no fires.

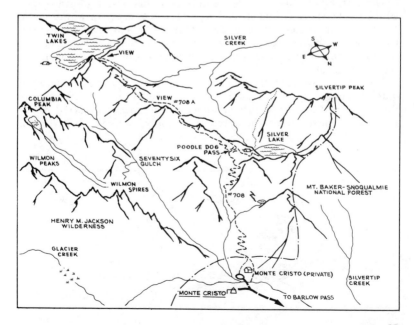

28 GLACIER BASIN

Round trip from Barlow Pass 13½ miles
Allow 2 days
High point 4500 feet

Elevation gain 2100 feet
Hikable July through October
USGS Monte Cristo and Blanca Lake

Meadows and boulders, flowers and snowfields, cold streams for wading and soft grass for napping, all in a dream basin tucked amid fierce peaks.

Until the flood of December 26, 1980, this was so short and popular a hike any observer could plainly see the eventual total devastation of the scene. The only salvation in sight was that popularity was generating unpopularity. Now the hike is long—too long for a rational day or even a relaxed weekend—and more glorious than it's been since the 1940s, when the automobile poked its nose into this valley. It would be a mad, mad world that reopened the road to Monte Cristo and thus rejected Mother Nature's gift.

Drive the Mountain Loop Highway 19.5 miles from the Verlot Public Service Center to Barlow Pass and park near the gated Monte Cristo road, elevation 2360 feet. (You may wish to call the Service Center to inquire about the road—see Hike 27.)

Walk the road 4⅓ miles, noting the many excellent spots to camp by the river. Introduce children to wilderness or basecamp for day hikes to high country. From the road split, 2800 feet, the right goes to Monte Cristo townsite and the Silver Lake trail. Climb left a short bit to Monte Cristo Campground and Glacier Basin trail No. 719. The start is on overgrown mining-logging road. At ½ mile is a wide swath of gravel and white water where Glacier Creek regularly goes crazy in winter, as in 1980; cross on temporary log bridges, marked by temporary plastic ribbons. (An alternate road-trail via Monte Cristo townsite bypasses this possible problem.) The road-trail continues 1 more mile to the end, now a scenic campsite.

The "true" trail commences at a moderate grade in open greenery but quickly plunges into Sitka alder and Alaska cedar and tilts straight up. Stop for a rest on a rock outcrop above a magnificent waterfall before tackling the next stretch, the worst, blisteringly hot and fly-bedeviled in

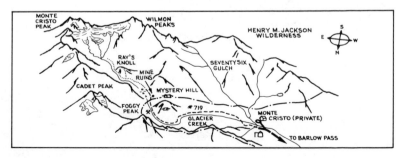

Glacier Basin

sunny summertime. The "trail" is so eroded by years of snowmelt and boots that were it not for the alder handholds, the rock slabs and mud walls would require mountaineering equipment. Going up, think how bad it's going to be coming *down*. But there's only ½ mile of the worst (an hour up, an hour down). The track then eases out in a gulch filled with talus, snow, and whistling marmots.

The difficulties are not quite over. When the water is high the trail is flooded and hikers must scramble over boulders. At 4500 feet, 2½ miles from Monte Cristo Campground, with startling abruptness the way opens into the basin—the meandering creeks, the flat fields of grass and blossoms, and the cliffs and glaciers of Cadet and Monte Cristo and Wilmon Peaks, the sharp thrust of Wilmon Spires.

What to do now? Sit and look, have lunch, watch the dippers. Or roam among boulders and wade sandy creeks and maybe organize a snowball fight. Or climb scree slopes to explore old mines. Or take a loitering walk to Ray's Knoll (named for climber Ray Rigg) and views over the basin and down the valley. Scramblers can continue up an easy gully to a higher cirque with glaciers, moraines, waterfalls, and broader views.

But please be kind to the basin meadows. Walk softly. And camp not in the flower fields but on a flat area partway up tree-covered Mystery Hill, to the right as you enter the basin. No fires!

29   GOAT FLATS

Round trip 9½ miles
Hiking time 6 hours
High point 4700 feet
Elevation gain 2000 feet

Hikable late July through
   October
One day or backpack
USGS Granite Falls and Silverton

    The rock spires and icefields of Three Fingers Mountain stand near the west edge of the North Cascades, rising above lowlands and saltwater (the Whulj, to use the name given it by the original residents), prominent on the skyline from as far away as Seattle. On a ridge of the mountain are the lovely alpine meadows of Goat Flats, the most beautiful in the Verlot area. Once upon a time a great network of trails linked the North and South Forks of the Stillaguamish River. Now most of the forest land is chopped up by logging roads, the trails ruined or abandoned or neglected. The hike to Goat Flats follows a small remnant of the old pedestrian network.

    Drive the Mountain Loop Highway 6.5 miles east from Granite Falls to Forest Service road No. 41 and turn left 1.5 miles to a major junction. Go left on road 41, passing several sideroads and also the Meadow Mountain trail (an alternate but longer route). At 18 miles from the Mountain Loop Highway turn right on road No. (4100)025 and in .2 mile find the trail-head, elevation 2800 feet.

    Trail No. 641 is a classic example of how tread can be completely worn out by the combined efforts of hiking feet and running water. The 2½ miles to Saddle Lake are all roots and rocks and gullies, such slow walking that to do them in less than 2 hours is to risk twisted ankles and broken legs. But take the better with the bitter; improving the trail would increase hiker traffic at Goat Flats, already severely overused. So

Goat Flats

walk carefully, slowly, blessing the roots and rocks and gullies or at least stifling your curses.

Just across the outlet of 3800-foot Saddle Lake is a junction. The trail to the right leads to campsites and a shelter on the far side of the lake and continues to Meadow Mountain a tree-covered hill. Go left to Three Fingers and Goat Flats.

From the lake the trail ascends steep slopes in forests to rolling meadows with acres and acres of blueberries and heather. The meadows are broken by groves of alpine trees and dotted with ponds—one in particular, several hundred feet below the trail, offers an excellent camp.

Some 2¼ miles from Saddle Lake the trail enters the meadow plateau of 4700-foot Goat Flats. Near the center is an historic artifact, an ancient log shelter once used as a patrol cabin, now serving as headquarters for local rodents. The meadows are paying the price of beauty, suffering badly from trampling. Visitors will want to leave the trail to pick blueberries and seek viewpoints but, as much as possible, should keep to beaten paths. Camping would better be done along the ridge before the flats; if here, it should be at existing sites. Fires are prohibited everywhere along the ridge.

For most hikers the flats are far enough, offering a close-up view of the cliffs and ice of Three Fingers, looks south to Pilchuck, north to Whitehorse and Mt. Baker, west to the Whulj and the Olympics. Campers get the best: sunsets on peaks and valleys, farm and city lights in the far-below lowland night, a perspective on megalopolis and wildness.

For hikers who want more, the trail goes on, traversing meadows and then climbing steeply up a rocky basin to 6400-foot Tin Can Gap, above the Three Fingers Glacier. From here a climbers' route weaves along an airy ridge to the foot of the pinnacle of the 6854-foot South Peak of Three Fingers, atop which is perched a lookout cabin built in the 1930s. The pinnacle is mounted by a series of ladders. In order to build the cabin the Forest Service dynamited a platform on the summit; tradition says the original summit never was climbed before it was destroyed. Tradition also says one lookout was so stricken by vertigo he had to telephone Forest Service supervisors to come help him down the ladder. Hikers will not want to go beyond Tin Can Gap.

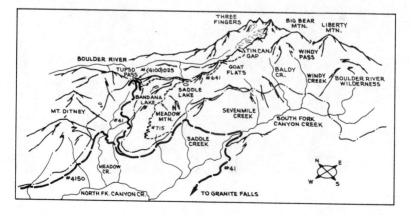

Lookout on top of Mount Pilchuck

30   MOUNT PILCHUCK

Round trip 4 miles
Hiking time 4 hours
High point 5324 feet
Elevation gain 2200 feet

Hikable late June to early
  November
One day
USGS Granite Falls

A peak at the very west edge of the range, prominent on the mountain horizon seen from the Whulj (as the original residents called the saltwater, *all* of the saltwater) and the lowlands, offering broad views west over farms, towns, cities, and Whulj to the Olympics and views east to the Cascades from Baker to Rainier.

Drive the Mountain Loop Highway east 1 mile from the Verlot Public Service Center. Turn right on Mt. Pilchuck State Park road No. 42 for 6.9 miles to the trailhead, a bit short of the road-end, elevation 3100 feet.

The trail ascends in gorgeous old-growth forest, then skirts the edge of a 1977 clearcut and switchbacks across the top of the ski slopes of the abandoned tow hill. Many confusing paths and many dabs of paint all lead to the same place.

The trail rounds the base of Little Pilchuck, climbing heather and ice-polished rock slabs to a saddle. The main route drops under a cliff and switchbacks ½ mile up southwest slopes to the summit. (A scramblers' route, marked with paint—which, incidentally, is an obnoxious way to smear up a mountain—goes straight up the ridge over huge blocks of granite.)

Views from the long-abandoned summit lookout cabin are magnificent —lowland civilization in one direction, mountain wilderness in the other. Immediately below sheer cliffs is Frozen Lake, set in a snowy and rocky cirque. For those with leftover energy, an easy way trail descends east along the ridge to a group of picturesque tarns perched on the ridge top.

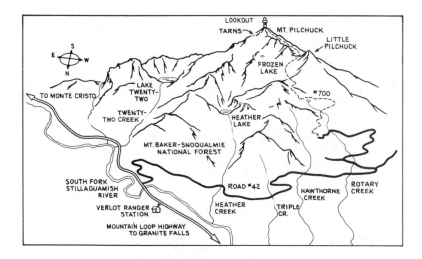

31   BALD MOUNTAIN

One-way trip about 9½ miles	Hikable July through October
Hiking time 6 hours	One day or backpack
High point 4500 feet	USGS Silverton and Index
Elevation gain from Stillaguamish	South Fork Stillaguamish River
2100 feet, from Sultan 1300 feet	

A fine high route traverses the 7-mile ridge separating Sultan Basin and the South Fork Stillaguamish River. Walk the complete way, partly in views of valleys, lakes, and peaks, and partly in deep forest. Or just visit the scenic climax—a dozen small lakes in huckleberry-heather meadows near the summit of 4851-foot Bald Mountain. This climax can be attained from either end. The distance is less from the Sultan start.

Stillaguamish start: Drive the Mountain Loop Highway from Granite Falls 4.5 miles past the Verlot Public Service Center and turn right on road No. 4020, signed "Bear Lake Trail" and "Bald Mountain Trail." At 2.3 miles from the highway turn right on road No. 4021, signed "Bald Mountain." In 1.5 miles more go left on road No. (4021)016 for .8 mile, dodging sideroads. At about 4.6 miles from the Loop Highway reach a large Department of Natural Resources sign and parking lot, elevation 2400 feet.

Walk a steep cat road up a few hundred feet to the trail, which proceeds from old clearcut into old virgin forest, much of the way on puncheon. At ¾ mile pass a sidetrail to Beaver Plant Lake and in a scant mile reach a Y. The right fork goes a short bit to Upper Ashland Lake and camps. Keep left.

The trail climbs around the end of Bald Ridge in grand forest, at 3 miles topping a 3950-foot saddle with views of Three Fingers, the Stillaguamish, and Clear Lake, directly below. At about 4 miles the trail, to pass under cliffs, switchbacks down and down 500 feet into the head of Pilchuck River; here is the first water since the lakes area. The lost elevation is regained and at about 6½ miles is a 4400-foot saddle under the highest peak of Bald Mountain. Here begin those promised meadows.

Sultan start: This end of the trail can be reached from either the town of Sultan or from Granite Falls as described here.

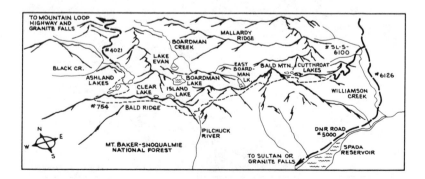

One of the Cutthroat Lakes

At the second stop sign in Granite Falls, turn right on South Alder Street. At .2 mile turn left on East Pioneer Street, signed "Lake Roesiger." At 4.5 miles turn left on DNR road No. 5000 (a large graveled road with a very small road sign). This road has numerous spurs so when in doubt look carefully for the signs. The road follows the Pilchuck River for miles and then switches from the Pilchuck to the Sultan River watershed. At 17 miles from Granite Falls pass the junction with the road to Sultan, which crosses Culmback Dam.

Stay on road 5000 (which may also be marked as Forest Service road No. 6126). The views become spectacular and the road steep. At 21 miles from Granite Falls cross Williamson Creek and at 22.5 miles turn left on DNR road No. 6100. Cross Williamson Creek again, and start climbing. At 1.7 miles from Williamson Creek keep left. At 2 miles leave SL-S-6100 and go right. At 2.6 miles reach a junction and the Bald Mountain parking area, elevation about 3200 feet.

Hike the road, switchbacking left, keeping to the right at the first spur and left at the second. At 1 mile the road ends and the foottrail enters forest. At 2 miles the forest becomes more alpine and at 2¾ miles from the parking lot the trail reaches a junction. The left fork contours around the south side of Bald Mountain 7 miles to Ashland Lakes as described above; the right fork drops a short mile to Cutthroat Lakes, a dozen or more delightful tarns and small lakes. There are plenty of campsites, but in late summer running water may be hard to find.

32 WHAT VERLOT FORGOT

Until the decades after World War II a trail network of some 50-odd miles radiated from the South Fork Stillaguamish River—Canyon Creek, Coal Creek, Bear Creek, Boardman Lakes, Mallardy Ridge, Granite Pass, and Everett's Boy Scout camp at Kelcema Lake. Logging roads obliterated many miles. More were abandoned when no longer needed by forest patrolmen or by the miners (prospectors) who built many of them. Less than half the near-Verlot mileage remains intact. A curious person might ask why this is so, considering that the crowds swarming on the "official" trails of the Verlot vicinity make them so overcrowded that a person pausing to sniff a flower is liable to get trampled.

Are you in a mood to be peaceful and quiet? Try the three abandoned trails noted here. Solitude is 99.9 percent guaranteed.

Mallardy Ridge

Round trip 5 miles
Hiking time 6 hours
High point 3800 feet
Elevation gain 1500 feet

Hikable June through October
One day
USGS Silverton

Of a 14-mile loop that started and ended at the river, 2½ miles along the top of Mallardy Ridge survive.

Drive the Mountain Loop Highway east 7.5 miles from the Verlot Public Service Center. Turn right on road No. 4030 for 6 miles to unmarked trail No. 705, located just where the road swings through a gap in the ridge, elevation 2800 feet.

Wiped out in places by clearcuts and never reestablished, the trail is easy to lose. If you do, go back and find it. It is extremely important to stay on the correct track (the correct ridge!). After the final clearcut the way becomes surprisingly free of blowdowns, easy to walk, following ups and downs of the crest. Climb off the trail to high points to see Sperry and Vesper Peaks and the red-rock south wall of Big Four Mountain.

Marten Creek

Round trip 5 miles
Hiking time 4 hours
High point 2800 feet
Elevation gain 1400 feet

Hikable June through October
One day
USGS Silverton

This surviving stretch of the old Granite Pass trail, which crossed to join the Kelcema Lake-Deer Pass trail, is a delightful walk through tall trees. The peaks tower. So does the brush!

Drive east 9.3 miles from the Verlot Public Service Center. A few feet beyond the Marten Creek bridge, find Marten Creek trail No. 713, elevation 1415 feet.

The first mile is on an abandoned, extremely steep mining road. At 1½ miles the trees thin and brush fills the gaps. Salmonberry, thimbleberry, devil's club, and vine maple grow waist high, shoulder high, and over your head. At about 2½ miles a small campsite beside Marten Creek is a good turnaround. The old mine apparently was across the creek, its secrets now guarded by jungle. At the valley head, Three Fingers Mountain can be seen poking its head over Granite Pass.

Marble Gulch

Round trip 6 miles
Hiking time 4 hours
High point 4200 feet
Elevation gain 1700 feet

Hikable June through September
One day
USGS Silverton

A tramway once carried ore from a mine at the headwaters of Williamson Creek up to and over Marble Pass and down to the Stillaguamish. The miners' trail began at Silverton and switchbacked under the tram to the pass, then proceeded 10 miles down to the Sultan River. Private property has blocked access from Silverton; a hiker therefore must wade the Stillaguamish River, only safely possible in late summer.

Drive the Mountain Loop Highway to within 1 mile of Silverton and find a suitable place to ford. On the far side scout around for the trail on the east side (left) of Marble Creek. Only bits and pieces of the original tread survive, but the route is walkable. The best views are a short way up the ridge above the pass.

View from Mallardy Ridge

33 PERRY CREEK— MOUNT FORGOTTEN

Round trip to meadows 8 miles
Hiking time 7 hours
High point 5200 feet
Elevation gain 3100 feet

Hikable mid-June through
   October
One day or backpack
USGS Bedal

A valley forest famed for its botanical richness, a waterfall, a small alpine meadow, and views of the impressive wall of Big Four Mountain and the white volcano of Glacier Peak. Come early for flowers, come late for blueberries.

Drive the Mountain Loop Highway east 15.2 miles from the Verlot Public Service Center. Just after crossing Perry Creek turn left on Perry Creek road No. 4063 for 1 mile to the road-end, elevation 2100 feet.

The trail traverses a steep hillside, now in forest, now in a grand display of ferns and flowers, boulder-hops a frenzied creek, and at 2 miles climbs above Perry Creek Falls. Pause to look over the top of the falls— but don't trust the handrail. A few feet farther the way crosses Perry Creek on boulders. A campsite is here.

Elevation is gained steadily in old-growth timber, which at 3½ miles yields to a small field of heather and lupine dotted by alpine trees. The trail switchbacks up forests on the slopes of Mt. Forgotten. Near the top of the switchbacks an abandoned trail branches off west, climbing to the ridge top near Stillaguamish Peak and dropping to South Lake. The main trail enters lush, fragile meadows and disappears at about 5200 feet, 4 miles.

Novice hikers should turn back here, well rewarded by views of Glacier Peak, seen at the head of the long valley of the White Chuck

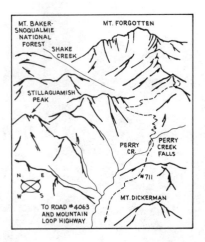

Deer ferns

Perry Creek Falls

River, and closer views of Big Four, Twin Peaks, Mt. Dickerman, and the long ridge of Stillaguamish Peak.

Experienced off-trail travelers can continue onward and upward a mile, climbing very steep heather slopes, then scrambling broken rock, to the 6005-foot summit of the peak and more views.

34 MOUNT DICKERMAN

Round trip 8½ miles
Hiking time 8–9 hours
High point 5723 feet
Elevation gain 3800 feet

Hikable late July through
  October
One day
USGS Bedal

All too few trails remain, outside wilderness areas and national parks, that begin in valley bottoms and climb unmarred forests to meadows. The way to Dickerman is strenuous, but the complete experience of life

October snowfall on Mount Dickerman. Del Campo Peak in distance

zones from low to high, plus the summit views, are worth every drop of sweat.

Drive the Mountain Loop Highway east 16.5 miles from the Verlot Public Service center to about 2.5 miles beyond Big Four Picnic Area, to a small parking area and easily overlooked trail sign, elevation 1900 feet.

Trail No. 710 doesn't fool around. Switchbacks commence instantly climbing up and up and up through lovely cool forest; except perhaps in late summer, several small creeks provide pauses that refresh. Tantalizing glimpses through timber give promise of scenery above. A bit past 2 miles lower-elevation trees yield to Alaska cedars and subalpine firs. Then the forest thins as the trail traverses under towering cliffs onto flatter terrain. Near here, in a sheltered hollow to the west, is a little lakelet produced by snowmelt and reached by a faint path; camping is possible.

The next ½ mile ranks among the most famous blueberry patches in the Cascades; in season, grazing hikers may find progress very slow indeed. In the fall, photographers find the blazing colors equally obstructive. Now, too, the horizons grow.

The final mile is somewhat steeper, switchbacking meadows to the broad summit, as friendly a sackout spot as one can find.

Abrupt cliffs drop toward Perry Creek forests, far below. Beyond are Stillaguamish Peak and Mt. Forgotten. To the east rise Glacier Peak, the horn of Sloan Peak, and all the Monte Cristo peaks. And across the South Fork Stillaguamish River are rugged Big Four Mountain and the striking rock slabs of Vesper Peak.

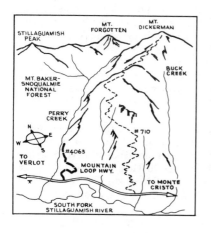

Picking blueberries

35 SUNRISE MINE TRAIL— HEADLEE PASS

Round trip 5 miles
Hiking time 5 hours
High point 4600 feet
Elevation gain 2500 feet

Hikable August and September
One day
USGS Silverton and Bedal

". . . . Theirs not to reason why, Theirs but to do and die: Into the valley of Death rode the six hundred. . . . "

Judging by the avalanche debris, the narrow valley ascended by the Sunrise Mine trail must be bombarded by snow, rock, and broken trees from the first snowfall in October until all the snow has slid from surrounding peaks sometime after mid-July. Hikers may feel they *are* the Light Brigade as they trudge into the valley, but if they make sure not to do so until the heavy artillery has ceased for the summer, the risk is no greater than on any other steep, rough, and often snow-covered terrain. The happy demise of the Monte Cristo road has put that area's several popular trails much deeper in de facto wilderness, glory be; as a consequence, more and more hikers with limited time have been finding the Sunrise Mine Trail on their own. Best that they (you) be warned what to expect.

Drive the Mountain Loop Highway east 17.1 miles from the Verlot Public Service Center toward (not to) Barlow Pass. Turn right on Sunrise Mine road No. 4065 for 2.3 miles to the road-end and trailhead, elevation 2100 feet. (The final ½ mile often is blocked by a slide.)

In the first ½ mile through forest the root-and-rock trail crosses four creeks, including—on a slippery log—the incipient South Fork Stillaguamish River. The second ½ mile, still rough, switchbacks steeply up a fern-covered hillside, rounds a corner, and levels briefly as the trail enters the steep, narrow valley of death or whatever.

Avalanche fans may remain unmelted all summer, or even for years. Just because you're technically "on" a trail don't be silly about steep, hard snow. Unless the way is clear, be satisfied with the valley view of peaks piercing the sky.

The miners who built the trail begrudged time that could be spent more entertainingly digging holes in the ground and sought to gain maximum elevation with minimum distance. No fancy-Dan 10-percent grade for *them*—the final mile, gaining 1200 feet to Headlee Pass, is 15–20 percent, ideal for hikers who also have no time to waste. The last 500 feet is in a slot gully where the grade has to be remade every summer by unpaid volunteers.

Headlee Pass, 4600 feet, is a thin cut in the ridge with rather limited views, confined by cliffs on three sides and snowy Vesper Peak to the east. The trail continues a short distance beyond the pass to an end at the edge of a giant rockslide; at one time it went to Sunrise Mine. A faint way trail crosses the slide to tiny Headlee Lake, often snowbound even at Labor Day.

Headlee Pass trail

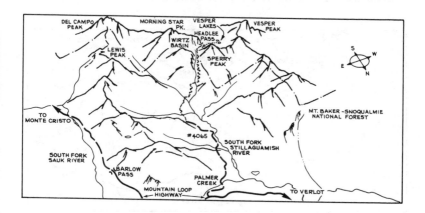

36 SULTAN BASIN D.N.R. TRAILS

Due to faulty mathematics when it entered the Union in 1889, Washington failed to obtain the full land grant due from the federal government. The error belatedly was noticed and the U.S. Forest Service handed over a large tract in the Mt. Pilchuck-Sultan River area. Even more belatedly, the state Department of Natural Resources commenced providing Forest Service-style recreational opportunities. Among the fruits of the new policy are two superb trails in the Sultan Basin leading to lovely subalpine lakes.

Drive US 2 to Sultan and on the east side of town turn left on a road signed "Sultan Basin Recreation Area." The sign is obscured and there is no turn lane; if you are unable to get off the highway—safely—on the first pass, try again, cautiously.

Drive Sultan Basin road 13 miles to Olney Pass, entry to the Everett Watershed. Visitors must register here. Car camping is forbidden in the watershed but not trail camping. However, be certain to use the toilet facilities so authorities will have no reason to prohibit backpackers.

Proceed a few feet from the pass to a three-way junction. Take the middle road, No. 61, and drive 7 miles to the Greider Lakes trailhead or 8.3 miles to the Boulder Lake trailhead.

Greider Lakes

Round trip 4 miles
Hiking time 3 hours
High point 2900 feet
Elevation gain 1400 feet

Hikable June through November
One day or backpack
USGS Index

Two delightful cirque lakes ringed by cliffs. Excellent campsites are at both. However, due to problems noted below, the trail is not recommended for little or timid or careless hikers.

Find the trail in a large parking area, elevation about 1500 feet. The path immediately enters forest, passes a picnic area and nature trail, and

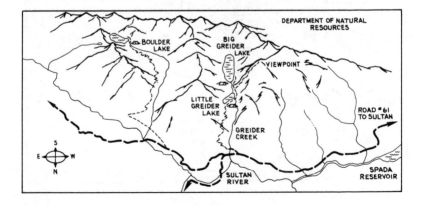

then starts climbing very steeply. "Defensive construction" technique was employed at the start to discourage motorcycles. The tread therefore is roughened by boulders and roots, infeasible for wheels and not easy for short-legged people. Near the top of the steep climb is a hazardous cliff scramble. At 2 miles, 2900 feet, reach Little Greider Lake and campsites. Cross the outlet stream and continue another ½ mile to Big Greider Lake and more campsites. Toilets at both lakes.

For greater views, go right near Big Greider Lake, climbing 600 feet in ¾ mile to a dramatic viewpoint.

Boulder Lake

Round trip 8 miles
Hiking time 5 hours
High point 3800 feet
Elevation gain 2400 feet

Hikable July through October
One day or backpack
USGS Index

The boulders are on the far side of the lake. The near side—the trail side—is meadows and forests and excellent campsites.

The trailhead, elevation 1600 feet, is on a badly eroded old logging road. The way begins with 1 mile, gaining 800 feet, on abandoned road. It moderates and becomes true though rough trail, crossing a brushy rockslide. Entering forest at 1½ miles, the tread improves as it switchbacks to a steep marsh at 3 miles, traversed on puncheon. At 4 miles is the lake, 3800 feet.

The camps are across the outlet stream on a heather hillside. Toilets are atop the knoll. Thick brush along the shores prevents an easy walk to the boulders on the far side.

Little Greider Lake

37   BLANCA LAKE

Round trip 8 miles
Hiking time 6–8 hours
High point 4600 feet
Elevation gain 2700 feet in, 600
feet out

Hikable July through October
One day or backpack
USGS Blanca Lake

The rugged cliffs of Kyes, Monte Cristo, and Columbia Peaks above, the white mass of the Columbia Glacier in the upper trough, and the deep waters of ice-fed Blanca Lake filling the lower cirque. A steep forest climb ending in grand views, with further explorations available to the experienced off-trail traveler.

Drive US 2 to Index junction and turn left on the North Fork Skykomish River road 14 miles to Garland Mineral Springs. At a junction .5 mile beyond the springs turn left on road No. 63 the 2 miles to Blanca Lake trail sign and parking area, elevation 1900 feet.

Trail No. 1052 immediately gets down to the business of grinding out elevation, relentlessly switchbacking up and up in forest, eventually with peeks out to Glacier Peak. At 3 miles the way reaches the ridge top at 4600 feet, the highest point of the trip, and at last enters the Henry M. Jackson Wilderness. In a few hundred yards is shallow little Virgin Lake, amid meadows and trees of a saddle on the very crest. Acceptable camping here for those who don't wish to carry packs farther, but no water in late summer.

Now the trail goes down, deteriorating into a mere route as it sidehills through trees with glimpses of blue-green water dropping 600 feet in 1 mile and reaching the 3972-foot lake at the outlet. Relax and enjoy the wind-rippled, sun-sparkling lake, ¾ mile long, the Columbia Glacier, the spectacular peaks. Where the trail hits the lake, and across the outlet stream on the west shore, are a number of overused but fairly decent campsites. No fires permitted; carry a stove.

Experienced hikers can explore along the rough west shore to the braided stream channels and waterfalls and flowers at the head of the lake. Those with proper mountaineering background and equipment can climb the Columbia Glacier to the col between Columbia and Monte Cristo Peaks and look down to Glacier Basin. The descent into the basin

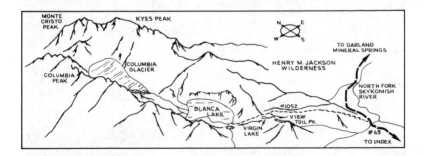

Air view of Blanca Lake and Kyes Peak

is not technically difficult, but strictly for parties skilled in use of the ice ax.

For a spectacular view of lake and mountains, hike to the top of 5128-foot Toil Peak, the first of two wooded bumps between Virgin Lake and Troublesome Mountain. On the highest point of the trail above Virgin Lake find a faint path traversing heather meadows southward, climbing at times steeply to the top.

Mount Rainier from Benchmark Mountain

SKYKOMISH RIVER
Henry M. Jackson Wilderness

38 WEST CADY RIDGE LOOP

Short loop trip 17 miles
Allow 2 days
High point 5816 feet
Elevation gain 3300 feet
**Hikable mid-July through late
 September**
**USGS Blanca Lake and
 Benchmark Mountain**

Long loop trip 23½ miles
Allow 2–3 days
Elevation gain 4700 feet

An easy loop through miles of forest and flower-covered alpine meadows, or a longer loop with more miles of forest and meadows. Both start on the North Fork Skykomish River trail and travel part of the way on the Pacific Crest National Scenic Trail. Both have a 1½-mile road walk to connect the beginning and end; if transportation can be arranged between the two trailheads, subtract 1½ miles and 500 feet of elevation gain from the trip log.

Except for West Cady Ridge, good campsites are scattered along the way. For the short loop, plan to camp high on Pass Creek. For the long loop, camp the first night 4 or 5 miles up the trail and the second night on the Crest Trail near Pass Creek.

Drive US 2 to Index junction and turn left on North Fork Skykomish River road 20 miles to the end and the North Fork Skykomish trailhead, elevation 3000 feet. Unload packs here and drive back 1.4 miles to where the loop will end at West Cady Ridge trailhead, elevation 2500 feet. Leave the car here and walk back up the road.

Hike 1½ miles on North Fork trail No. 1051 to the junction with Pass Creek trail No. 1053, signed "Cady Pass 3½ miles," elevation 3200 feet.

For the short loop, go right, crossing the North Fork on a footlog, then climbing a sometimes muddy and brushy trail to the Pacific Crest Trail, 5 miles from the road, 4200 feet. Find campsites on the Crest Trail just after crossing Pass Creek.

For the long loop, back at the Pass Creek junction continue up the North Fork trail on sometimes excellent and sometimes poor tread. At about 4 miles from the road cross the North Fork Skykomish River on a footlog to a nice campsite. At 5 miles the path traverses a large huckleberry parkland with water and camping space. From here the way climbs to Dishpan Gap and the Pacific Crest Trail, 7½ miles from the road, 5600 feet.

Head south on the Crest Trail (Hike 52) 4 miles through beautiful alpine meadows, passing Wards Pass and Lake Sally Ann to Cady Pass; ½ mile beyond the pass join the short loop at Pass Creek, 4200 feet.

From Pass Creek continue south on the Crest Trail 2¼ miles and go right on West Cady Ridge trail No. 1054, 4900 feet. Here begin the 4 glorious miles of meadows. Be sure to take in the highest point of the ridge, 5816-foot Benchmark Mountain, surrounded by fields of heather and flowers and horizons of views, including Sloan Peak, the Monte Cristo peaks, Glacier, Baker, and Rainier.

A delightful walk in alpine meadows follows the ups and downs of 4-mile-long West Cady Ridge. At its abrupt end the trail descends a series of short switchbacks, 8 miles from the Crest Trail, reaching the North Fork a short distance from the road-end.

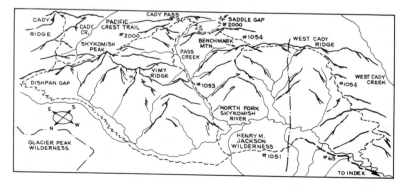

39 BARCLAY AND EAGLE LAKES

Round trip to Eagle Lake 8½ miles
Hiking time 6 hours
High point 3888 feet
Elevation gain 1700 feet

Hikable late June through
  October
One day or backpack
USGS Baring

For many years Barclay Lake was among the most popular low-elevation hikes in the Cascades, passing through pleasant old forest to the base of the tremendous north wall of Mt. Baring, a good trip in early spring and late fall when higher country was deep in snow. The wall remains, and the lake, but not much forest. Tragically, the walk to Barclay Lake no longer deserves, by itself, inclusion in this book. However, there is still Eagle Lake, amid trees, meadows, and peaks, and offering a staggering cross-valley look at the north wall of Baring, a legend among climbers and to date ascended only once.

Drive US 2 some 6 miles east from Index junction. Turn left at Baring on 635 Place NE, cross railroad tracks, and go 4.3 miles on road No. 6024 to the trailhead, elevation 2200 feet.

The trail, with minor ups and downs and numerous mudholes, meanders through what remains of the forest of Barclay Creek, in 1½ miles reaching Barclay Lake, 2422 feet, and at 2¼ miles ending near the inlet stream. Camping is possible at several spots along the shore. Enjoy the neck-stretching look up and up the precipice of 6123-foot Baring Mountain.

At the lakehead, just where the trail leaves the water by a small campsite, find a meager path climbing 1000 feet straight up steep forest. For a bit the way is on rockslide, then briefly levels and resumes climbing beside another rockslide. The grade abruptly flattens at a viewpoint above Stone Lake and contours to 3888-foot Eagle Lake.

By the shore is a private cabin, kept locked; the owner maintains a campsite for public use near the outlet.

For more views, and for meadows, wander up the easy slopes of 5936-

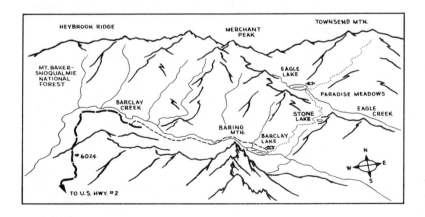

Merchant Peak from Eagle Lake

foot Townsend Mountain, or from the outlet roam downstream through the lovely forest, heather, and marsh of Paradise Meadow.

Now then. As you are sitting in Paradise Meadow nursing bruises and sprains and wiping sweat from your eyes, you may be hailed by a fisherman who is astounded at your suffering and stupidity, inasmuch as he is just a half-hour from his car, parked on a logging road up Eagle Creek. And you go home and write a letter demanding to know why this guidebook has put you through this ordeal. Well, what makes it an ordeal is not the steep climb, which enriches the wilderness experience, but learning a road is so near (though not by trail—it's a brush route). Why isn't the road gated, banning public vehicles, and thus placing Eagle Lake back in deep wilderness where it belongs?

Meadows on side of Scorpion Mountain

40 SCORPION MOUNTAIN

Round trip 9 miles
Hiking time 6 hours
High point 5540 feet
Elevation gain 2300 feet in, 300 feet out

Hikable July through October
One day
USGS Evergreen Mountain and Captain Point

Looking for views from an easy trail? Try Evergreen Mountain. Looking for a pleasant family walk? Choose any other destination but Scorpion! Even the access road, carved into a steep hillside stripped bare of trees, is difficult. And there is no water on the path, making at least one loaded canteen essential. However, hikers seeking solitude and a nice view at the end of a tough trail will find Scorpion just their cup of tea.

Drive US 2 to Skykomish. Just beyond town turn left on Beckler River road No. 65. At 7 miles turn right on road No. 6520, signed "Johnson Creek" and "Johnson Ridge Trail." At 1.7 miles from Beckler River road keep straight ahead at a junction and at 5.6 miles turn right on No. 6526 to its end, elevation 3600 feet. If the going is too hairy, park and walk the last mile.

Trail No. 1067 begins with ½ mile of abandoned road. Keep left at a switchback, reaching real trail at ¾ mile, on the ridge top.

The seldom-used trail was cleared in 1967 in the process of fighting a series of little fires, all fortunately extinguished before reaching proportions of the devastating Evergreen Mountain fire which occurred at the same time. The trail is obscured here and there by windfalls but there is no problem detouring around them. If the tread is lost, just follow the ridge top.

The heavily wooded ridge crest occasionally offers glimpses of rocky 6190-foot Mt. Fernow to the south. At 2¼ miles the trail passes over the top of 5056-foot Sunrise Mountain, with a view of Glacier Peak, and then drops about 300 feet before climbing nearly to the top of 5540-foot Scorpion Mountain at 4 miles. Leave the path at its highest point and follow the ridge a few hundred feet to the summit, flanked by a lush carpet of grass and flowers and surrounded by a panorama of the Cascades.

The trail continues around the southern shoulder of the mountain and drops 500 feet to tiny Joan Lake at 4½ miles.

Volunteers are reopening 5½ miles of an old trail from Scorpion Mountain to Captain Point and Scenic.

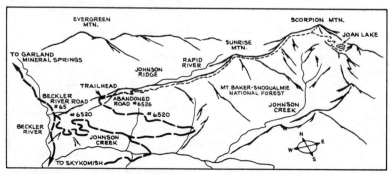

41 A PEACH, A PEAR, AND A TOPPING

Round trip to Pear Lake 15 miles
Allow 2 days
High point 5300 feet
Elevation gain 3200 feet in, 500 feet out

Hikable July through October
USGS Captain Point and Benchmark Mountain

Savor flower and heather gardens ringing three alpine lakes and a spatter of ponds along the Pacific Crest Trail. And if all these sweet things seem to call for whipped cream, stroll to a peak for the panorama of a horizon full of valleys and mountains.

To approach from the east, drive road No. 6701 from the Little Wenatchee River (see Hike 50) and at 4 miles past the junction with road No. (6701)400 find Top Lake trail No. 1506. From the more popular west, drive US 2 to Skykomish and just east of town turn north on Beckler River road No. 65. At 7 miles turn right on Rapid River road No. 6530. At 11.4 miles is the start of Meadow Creek trail No. 1057, elevation 2100 feet.

Beginning amid the ravages of the 1967 Evergreen Mountain fire and subsequent salvage logging, the trail (a goshawful goo from churning by horses, which also ruined hillside tread) gains almost 1000 feet switchbacking out of Rapid River valley. At about 1 mile the burn is left, forest entered, and the grade moderates and contours into Meadow Creek drainage, crossing Meadow Creek at 3 miles by hopping boulders (there aren't really enough). At 3¾ miles recross the creek to a junction with an abandoned trail to West Cady Ridge. The way climbs steeply from Meadow Creek into West Cady Creek drainage. At 6½ miles reach the lower of the two Fortune Ponds, 4700 feet, and an intersection with the old Crest Trail.

Walk south. At 7¾ miles cross 5200-foot Frozen Finger Pass between West Cady Creek and Rapid River and drop to Pear Lake, 8 miles, 4809 feet. Do not camp within 200 feet of the shores here or at Fortune Ponds. The meadows are so fragile, and so damaged, you really ought to sling a hammock in the trees. Peach Lake, at the same elevation over the ridge south, is best reached by contouring off trail around the ridge end and be-

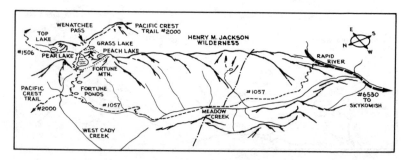

low cliffs, passing narrow Grass Lake. Top Lake is attained via ½ mile more on the Crest Trail and another ½ mile on trail No. 1506. For the promised land of views, leave the trail at Fortune Ponds and ascend Fortune Mountain, 5903 feet.

(Above) Upper Fortune Pond
(Below) Bear tracks on shore of upper Fortune Pond

42 WHAT SKYKOMISH FORGOT

Some of the largest alpine meadows in the Skykomish area lie along abandoned and forgotten trails. Until the 1950s a pedestrian network of 50 miles radiated from the Beckler River east to the Cascade Crest— Evergreen Mountain, Beckler Peak, Alpine Baldy, Scorpion Mountain, around Captain Point, Valhalla Mountain to the Pacific Crest Trail, and the Martin Creek-Kelley Creek trail to Scorpion Mountain. When loggers needed room for their trucks and forest rangers quit walking, fewer than 20 miles were left intact, and they were let go back to nature. However, except where roads and clearcuts have reduced Creation to a condition resembling that sometime between the Third Day and the Fifth, the tread is still there, just waiting for the pioneer-minded and the solitude fanatics.

Alpine Baldy

Round trip 4 miles
Hiking time 4 hours
High point 5200 feet
Elevation gain 1600 feet

Hikable late June through October
One day
USGS Captain Point, Scenic, Skykomish

Drive US 2 east 3.3 miles from Skykomish and turn left on road No. 66. In 6.6 miles keep right (straight ahead) on road No. 6610 for 4.4 more

Alpine meadows on North Crest Cutoff Trail

miles to the end of maintained road, elevation about 3600 feet.

Walk the abandoned road to its very end and climb straight up, first in clearcut, then woods, to the ridge. With or without trail, ascend the ridge in forest to the summit of Alpine Baldy, 5200 feet. No views here. Turn left on a well-preserved trail that descends to the edge of a large, steep meadow and then climbs to a 5100-foot high point with stupendous views.

Kelley Creek

Round trip 8 miles
Hiking time 6 hours
High point 5000 feet
Elevation gain 2000 feet

Hikable late June through
October
One day
USGS Captain Point, Scenic,
Skykomish

Drive US 2 east 6 miles from Skykomish and just opposite milepost 55 turn left on road No. 67, signed "Old Cascade Road." At 2.2 miles from the highway go left on road No. 6710. At 5.6 miles from the highway go left again, on road No. 6720, for .5 mile to the road-end, elevation about 3200 feet.

Walk the overgrown road through a clearcut to the end. Bushwhack a short way up to unmolested forest and contour the steep bank overlooking Kelley Creek. Poke about for the faint tread, which is not too hard to find but is difficult to stay on, especially in brush.

The trail splits in a large heather meadow, 5000 feet, below Captain Point. The left fork goes to Scorpion Mountain (Hike 40); the right is the North Crest Cutoff Trail (below).

North Crest Cutoff Trail

Round trip 4 miles
Hiking time 4 hours
High point 5409 feet
Elevation gain 750 feet in, 350 feet
out

Hikable late June through
October
One day
USGS Captain Point, Scenic,
Skykomish

The North Crest Cutoff Trail extends 8 miles from Scorpion Mountain to the Pacific Crest Trail near Lake Janus. It is intersected by road No. 6710, giving a choice of a hike west or a hike east.

Drive road No. 6710 (see Kelley Creek, above) 7.6 miles to a ridge top. Go right for the hike east. For the west, turn left .6 mile to the road-end, elevation 4850 feet.

Ascend the clearcut ridge to forest and find the faint tread. The trail used to contour a huge, steep meadow but with abandonment came sloughing and slipperiness; until tread is restored, stay on the ridge crest, climbing (at times steeply) on a well-traveled track over two high points. At the second, 5409 feet, is a helipad. Overgrown trail descends to a heather meadow and a junction with the Kelley Creek and Scorpion Mountain trails.

Lake Valhalla from Pacific Crest Trail

NASON CREEK
Partly in Henry M. Jackson Wilderness

 LAKE VALHALLA

Round trip 11 miles
Hiking time 6 hours
High point 5100 feet
Elevation gain 1100 feet in, 400 feet out

Hikable mid-July through October
One day or backpack
USGS Labyrinth Mountain

North from Stevens Pass the Pacific Crest Trail roams by a succession of meadowy alpine lakes. First in line is Lake Valhalla, set in a cirque under the cliffs of Lichtenberg Mountain.

Drive US 2 to Stevens Pass, elevation 4061 feet, and park in the lot at the east end of the summit area. Find the trail beside the utility substation.

The way begins along the original grade of the Great Northern Railroad, used when trains went over the top of the pass; the right-of-way was abandoned upon completion of the first Cascade Tunnel (predecessor of the present tunnel) early in the century.

From the open hillside, views extend beyond the pass to ski slopes and down Stevens Creek to Nason Creek and far east out the valley. Below is the roar of highway traffic. In 1½ miles the gentle path rounds the end of the ridge and enters the drainage of Nason Creek.

The main trail descends a bit to cross a little stream, climbs a ridge, and at 3½ miles enters a basin of meadows and marsh, with a fine campsite. Staying east and below the Cascade Crest, the way ascends easily to a 5100-foot spur, then drops to the rocky shore of the 4830-foot lake.

Heavily used and frequently crowded camps lie among trees near the inlet. The best sites are near the outlet, where the terrain is less fragile. No fires are permitted, of course; carry a stove. For explorations climb heather meadows to the summit of 5920-foot Lichtenberg and broad views or continue north on the Pacific Crest Trail (Hike 100) as far as time and energy allow.

A much shorter (5½ miles round trip) but less scenic approach is via the Smith Brook trail (Hike 44) which joins the Pacific Crest Trail at Union Gap 1 mile from the road. The Crest Trail leads south from the Gap 1¾ miles to Lake Valhalla.

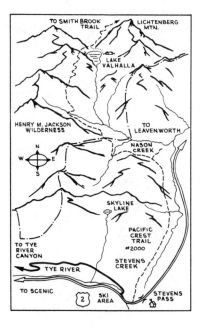

Pipsissewa or prince's pine

44 LAKE JANUS AND GRIZZLY PEAK

Round trip to Grizzly Peak 17 miles
Hiking time 6–8 hours
High point 5597 feet
Elevation gain 2200 feet in, 800 feet out

Hikable mid-July through October
One day or backpack
USGS Labyrinth Mountain and Captain Point

A beautiful alpine lake and a long ridge trail, sometimes in Western Washington and sometimes in Eastern Washington and sometimes straddling the fence. An easy but spectacular stretch of the Pacific Crest Trail. The trip can be done in a day, but at least a weekend should be planned—the lake is inviting and so is "looking around the next corner."

Drive US 2 east 4.5 miles from Stevens Pass and turn left on Smith Brook road No. 6702. Cross Nason Creek bridge, turn left, and follow the road 3.5 miles toward Rainy Pass to the Smith Brook trailhead, elevation 3800 feet. (Parking is precarious on the narrow road here and is better done on the switchback below.)

Climb 1 mile on trail No. 1590 to 4680-foot Union Gap and the junction with the Pacific Crest Trail. Turn right, dropping 700 feet down the west side of the crest to round cliffs of Union Peak, then regaining part of the elevation before reaching 4146-foot Lake Janus, 2½ miles from the gap. The trail goes through pleasant forest in the far-off sound of Rapid River. Though the grade is gentle the tread is badly eroded in places.

The lake is everything an alpine lake should be—sparkling water surrounded by meadows and tall trees and topped by the bright green slopes of 6007-foot Jove Peak. Numerous camps are available, but finding one vacant is a rare chance on weekends. Those near the shore have been closed for rehabilitation. Forget wood fires; carry a stove.

From the lake the trail enters forest on smooth and easy tread, climbs 1100 feet in 1½ miles to the Cascade Crest (good camps here), contours around the Eastern Washington side of a small hill, and ducks around a

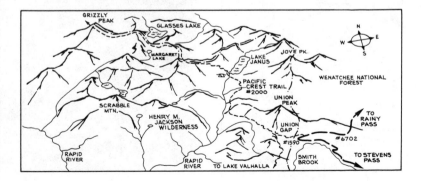

corner back to Western Washington, a process repeated frequently on the way to Grizzly Peak. Carry water; there's little along the way.

Every turn of the crest-wandering trail offers new views. Look east down into Lake Creek and Little Wenatchee River drainage and across to nearby Labyrinth Mountain. Look north to Glacier Peak. Look west down to the Rapid River and out to peaks above the Skykomish. At 2½ miles from Lake Janus is a glimpse of Margaret Lake, some 400 feet below the trail. A short ½ mile beyond is a view down to Glasses Lake and larger Heather Lake; this is a good turnaround point for day hikers.

At about 5¼ miles from Lake Janus the trail climbs within a few feet of the top of 5597-foot Grizzly Peak and more panoramas. The trail also goes close to the summit of a nameless peak with a view of Glacier Peak; succumbing to this temptation will lead to further temptations on and on along the Pacific Crest Trail.

Lake Janus

NASON RIDGE

One-way trip 16 miles
Allow 2–3 days
High point 6400 feet
Elevation gain 4500 feet

Hikable mid-July through
October
USGS Wenatchee Lake

The magnificent 26-mile journey the full length of Nason Ridge, through forest and wide-sky highlands from near the Pacific Crest Trail to near Lake Wenatchee, is a prime tour for experienced navigators. Unfortunately, the first 5 miles from Rainy Pass to Snowy Creek have never been built and the last 6½ miles to Lake Wenatchee are so muddled up with logging roads and harassed by motorcycles as to be no fun; the 16 miles between Snowy Creek and Round Mountain road, though, are superb.

The trip can best be done with two cars. Leave one at the Snowy Creek trailhead (Hike 46), elevation 3500 feet, and drive to the Round Mountain trailhead (Hike 49), elevation 4100 feet.

Climb a steep 1000 feet in 1½ miles to the junction with Nason Ridge trail No. 1583 on Round Mountain and go left up a wooded ridge to within ¼ mile of 6227-foot Alpine Lookout (well worth the detour). From the lookout the trail drops to Merritt Lake (Hike 48) and campsites, 9 miles from the start.

Still in timber, the trail continues downward. In 1 mile keep right at a junction with the Merritt Lake trail. Ascend forest to a 5400-foot high point and drop to a crossing of Royal Creek and campsites at 4900 feet. Now the way climbs into meadowland, passing tiny Crescent Lake, 5500 feet, to a 6000-foot high point and skirting Rock Lake to a junction with the Rock Mountain trail (Hike 47), 12 miles from the car. Camp in established sites in the trees near Crescent and Rock Lakes and not in the fragile meadows surrounding them.

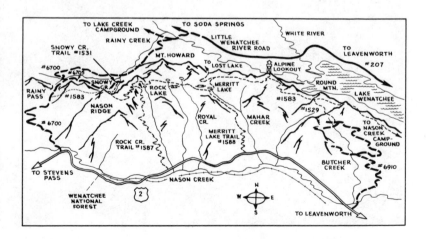

An endless number of small switchbacks take the trail to a 6400-foot shoulder of Rock Mountain, followed by a final drop to the Snowy Creek trailhead.

Rock Lake

Head of Snowy Creek Basin

NASON CREEK
Unprotected area

46   SNOWY CREEK-ROCK MOUNTAIN

Round trip 9 miles
Hiking time 6 hours
High point 6852 feet
Elevation gain 3350 feet

Hikable mid-July through
   October
One day or backpack
USGS Wenatchee Lake

Forest, meadows, and switchbacks through the sky lead to the summit of Rock Mountain. This is a much more civilized route than the Rock Mountain trail (Hike 47). It starts 900 feet higher and has cool shade for hours after the other is so hot you can hear the ants sizzling.

Drive US 2 east 4.5 miles from Stevens Pass and turn left on Smith Brook road No. 6700 (Hike 41). Cross Rainy Pass and about 5 miles from the highway, at a major switchback, go straight ahead on road No. 6705 another 3.5 miles to a crossing of Snowy Creek and the trailhead, elevation 3500 feet.

Snowy Creek trail No. 1531 proceeds beyond a 1974 clearcut into magnificent old-growth forest. At 2 miles, 3800 feet, is a fine campsite in upper Snowy Creek Basin, a large meadow flat enclosed by a horseshoe of cliffy peaks. Tread vanishes in the meadow, then reappears halfway across, on the left. The next 2 miles (steep and dry) enter trees, leave them for flower fields, and gain 1800 feet to the summit ridge of Rock Mountain. Here is a junction with the Nason Ridge-Rock Mountain trail. Go left on the crest to the lookout site atop Rock Mountain, 6852 feet, and the glorious views described in Hike 47.

(Opposite) View from top of Rock Mountain

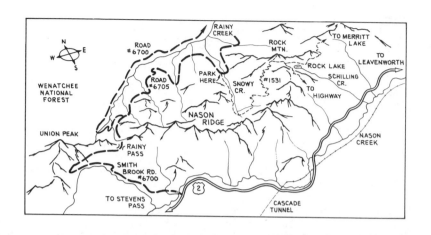

47 ROCK MOUNTAIN

Round trip 11 miles
Hiking time 8 hours
High point 6852 feet
Elevation gain 4250 feet

Hikable mid-July through
  October
One day or backpack
USGS Wenatchee Lake

Broad meadows and a cold little lake enhance Rock Mountain, the scenic climax of Nason Ridge. However, the person who chooses this route to the top, rather than Snowy Creek (Hike 46), must be young and stubborn or old and ornery. The trail is very steep, despite 95 switchbacks. It lies on a south slope swept clean of shade trees by fire and avalanche. No water—unless you swallow a few thousand of the flies which, in season, fling themselves into your gasping mouth.

Coming from the east, drive US 2 east 9.4 miles from Nason Creek Rest Area. From the west, cross Stevens Pass and drive .4 mile past the Highway Department buildings. Near milepost 73 find a small parking area and the Rock Mountain trail sign, elevation 2600 feet.

Rock Mountain trail No. 1587 begins on a powerline service road. In about ⅓ mile go left, climbing steeply to the highest powerline pylon at about ⅔ mile, 3000 feet.

True trail commences, narrow and rocky, switchbacking up the naked bones of the mountain. Views, of course, begin immediately and never quit. The massive high bulk of the Chiwaukum Mountains, across the valley, dominates. A bit to the west, the green slopes of Arrowhead Mountain and Jim Hill Mountain grow greener the higher you climb. At about 3½ miles, 5000 feet, the wayside vegetation shifts to the subalpine—blueberries, heather, and shrubby Christmas trees (mighty thin shade). At 4½ miles, 6000 feet, is a junction with the Nason Ridge trail.

For Rock Lake turn right on the ridge trail, contouring several hundred feet above the lake. The snowfields that generally fill the basin until late July may be mighty tempting to feet that have been frying for hours on the sunny side of the ridge. Don't camp in the fragile meadows by the lake inlet. Find nice sites in the trees just above and to the northeast of the shore.

For Rock Mountain turn left on the ridge trail, switchbacking, then

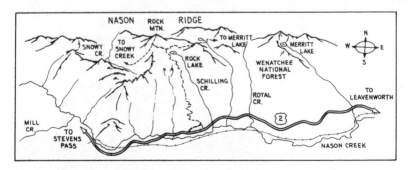

Rock Mountain trail

following a spur ridge, and switchbacking again to the summit ridge and a junction with the Snowy Creek trail (Hike 46). Steep snow may force a party to detour or call it a day or call Mountain Rescue.

The summit ridge is an easy walk to the old lookout site atop Rock Mountain, 6852 feet, 5½ miles from the highway. The views extend north to Sloan Peak and Glacier Peak, south to the tip of Mt. Rainier rising above Mt. Daniel, and straight down 1000 feet to Rock Lake.

MERRITT LAKE

Round trip 6 miles
Hiking time 4 hours
High point 5003 feet
Elevation gain 2000 feet

Hikable late June through
**   October**
One day or backpack
USGS Wenatchee Lake

Merritt Lake is a delightful tarn ringed by subalpine forest and enclosed by 6000-foot peaks. Fishermen, botanizers, and esthetes swarm. Nearby is another popular lake—the largest on Nason Ridge—that goes

Merritt Lake

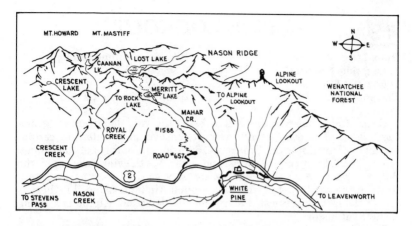

by the name of "Lost." Some hikers do indeed become lost, and wounded, too, because the trail is difficult and treacherous, definitely not for the inexperienced wayfarer.

Coming from the east, drive US 2 west 6 miles from Nason Creek Rest Area. From the west, drive east 11 miles from Stevens Pass to 3.3 miles beyond the Highway Department buildings. Near milepost 76 turn north on road No. 657 for 1.6 miles to the road-end and the start of Merritt Lake trail No. 1588, elevation 3000 feet.

The trail switchbacks up through a scattering of splendid old Ponderosa pine and Douglas fir. At 2 miles skirt a boulder field and cross a small creek. At 2½ miles is a junction with Nason Ridge trail No. 1583 (Hike 45) and at 3 miles, Merritt Lake, 5003 feet. Numerous camps lie in the woods, handy to an open-air privy. Campers will want to carry a stove; the scene was picked clean of good burning wood by fishermen a couple of generations ago.

For Lost Lake, follow the Nason Ridge trail up and away from Merritt Lake a very scant ½ mile to a junction. The ridge trail ascends right to Alpine Lookout. Go left on the unmarked Lost Lake trail, climbing to a 5500-foot pass and then descending, initially at an easy grade but soon in a steep and slippery draw, sharing the trail with a creek. People with slippery shoes and a tendency to break bones easily shouldn't try it. The route is straight down to the lake, 4930 feet. Aside from fish, there are views up to 6800-foot Mt. Masstiff. Camps are located around the outlet. Keep in mind the 650-foot climb on the return; add 3 miles and 3 hours to the round trip.

49 ALPINE LOOKOUT

Round trip 10 miles
Hiking time 5 hours
High point 6237 feet
Elevation gain 2300 feet

Hikable mid-June through
  September
One day
USGS Wenatchee Lake

Nason Ridge has a reputation as being the very definition of "grueling." That, of course, is only accurate insofar as it refers to certain stretches of certain trails. This route, for example, hardly gets up enough sweat for a hiker to notice there is no water. Yet the views are broad, the flowers pretty. Moreover, chances are very good of spotting mountain goats in the small no-hunting area around Alpine Lookout. Further, as one of the last lookouts still active for fire detection, Alpine is a living vignette of history.

Drive US 2 east 17 miles from Stevens Pass to Nason Creek Rest Area and a few hundred feet beyond. Pass a private driveway and turn left on Butcher Creek road No. 6910. Cross Nason Creek, avoid spur roads, and at 2½ miles turn right, staying on road No. 6910 to Round Mountain trail No. 1529, elevation 3900 feet.

The first 1½ miles are typically "Nason," climbing steeply to meet Nason Ridge trail No. 1583, 5300 feet. Go left. The next 3 miles are also less than perfect joy because the Forest Service currently gives motorcycles free run to the lookout junction. The trail (wheel road) contours the side of Round Mountain and gains almost 1000 feet to the junction. A short wheelfree spur leads to Alpine Lookout, 6237 feet, 5 miles from the road.

The views are north to cliffs of Dirtyface Mountain, above waters of Lake Wenatchee, and south to the Stuart Range, Chiwaukum Mountains, and other peaks of the Alpine Lakes Wilderness.

The best times to see goats are early and late in the day. Don't wander about searching. Sit still, be quiet, and wait for them to come near you. Don't visit the lookout sanctuary during hunting season, when your presence might frighten the animals out of their small safe spot into the rifle sights.

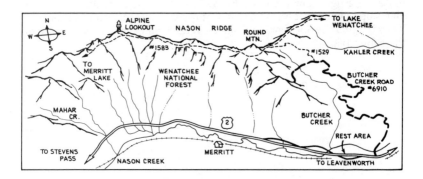

Mountain goat in protected area near Alpine Lookout

Theseus Lake

LITTLE WENATCHEE RIVER
Henry M. Jackson Wilderness

50 MINOTAUR LAKE

Round trip 6 miles
Hiking time 5 hours
High point 5500 feet
Elevation gain 2000 feet

Hikable mid-July through
October
One day or backpack
USGS Labyrinth Mountain

Minotaur Lake lies in a Grecian setting. Above and beyond are the rock walls of 6376-foot Labyrinth Mountain. Below is Theseus Lake. Heather meadows and alpine firs complete the mythological scene. No longer are seven girls and seven boys annually given in sacrifice to Minotaur, but each year visitors pay (in season) a tribute to the gods as the bugs take a libation of blood.

Drive US 2 east from Stevens Pass 19 miles and turn left to Lake

128

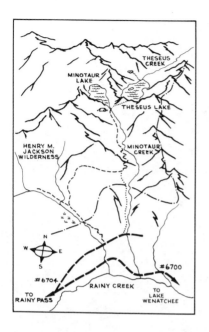

Cow parsnip

Wenatchee. Pass the state park road, the roads to Plain and Fish Lake, and continue to Lake Wenatchee Ranger Station and 1.5 miles beyond to a junction. Go left on Little Wenatchee River road No. 65 for 6 miles, then turn left again, cross the river first on road No. 6702 then No. 6700 for 8 miles, then go right on road No. 6704 (this junction also can be reached from the Smith Brook–Rainy Pass road No. 6702, Hike 44) and 1 more mile to the trailhead, elevation 3800 feet. (Note: the trailhead is scheduled to be relocated ¼ mile down the road.)

The way begins on North Fork Rainy Creek trail, which is combined with Minotaur Lake trail No. 1517, maintained but muddy. The trail switchbacks up a hill, drops to cross an unnamed creek, and follows this stream ¾ mile. At about 1 mile the way becomes a mere fishermen's path shooting straight up. There is no formal tread, only the groove pounded by many boots, gaining 1500 feet in the next mile. Views are limited to a few glimpses out through trees. At the end of the long, steep, dry ascent the trail turns downvalley ½ mile, losing 100 feet, then turns again and heads up Minotaur Creek. Forest gives way to highland meadows and at 3 miles is 5550-foot Minotaur Lake.

In trees around the shore are several good campsites, a mob scene on weekends. Carry a stove; the last good firewood was burned up in 1937. Cross the outlet and walk a few yards northeast to see 5060-foot Theseus Lake; a very steep path leads down to more good camps and the shores of the lake.

For broader views of mountains west to Stevens Pass, north to Glacier Peak, and east beyond Lake Wenatchee, scramble easily to open ridges above the lakes and wander the crests.

51 HEATHER LAKE

Round trip 6½ miles
Hiking time 4 hours
High point 3953 feet
Elevation gain 1300 feet

Hikable July through October
One day or backpack
USGS Labyrinth Mountain and
Captain Point

Waters of the ½-mile-long lake-in-the-woods reflect rocks and gardens of Grizzly Peak. A family could be happy here for days, prowling about from a comfortable basecamp. So could doughty adventurers seeking more strenuous explorations. The bad news is that on summer weekends it's often impossible to find a campsite.

From the upper end of Lake Wenatchee (Hike 50), drive 6 miles on Little Wenatchee River road No. 65, turn left on road No. 6702, cross the river, and in .5 mile go right on road No. 6701, following the river upstream. In 4.7 miles turn left onto road No. (6701)510. In 300 feet keep right and in another 2.3 miles reach the trailhead at the road-end, elevation 2700 feet. This trail also can be reached from the east side of Stevens Pass on road No. 6702, signed "Smith Brook Road" (Hike 44), a 12-mile dirt road climbing over 4600-foot Rainy Pass to road No. 6701 near the Little Wenatchee River.

The trail is a constant joy (nearly). The minor ups and downs of the first 1½ miles, netting only 100 feet, ease muscles into their task. Having done so, it turns stern, crossing Lake Creek on a bridge and heading up seriously, leaving no doubt why horses are forbidden. At 1½ miles is the boundary of the Henry M. Jackson Wilderness. In 2½ miles, after gaining 900 feet, the grade relents and joy resumes in the last ¾ mile to Heather Lake, 3953 feet, with fine camps and a cozy privy.

The bare schist near the lake outlet displays the grinding done by the glacier that scooped out the lake basin. Once these slabs were smooth, but eons of erosion have eaten away the polish, leaving only the grooves.

Attractive to the ambitious navigator with USGS map and compass, a way trail rounds the left side of the lake. At the far end follow a small stream south, climbing 700 feet in ½ mile to Glasses Lake, 4626 feet, so named because from neighboring peaks it looks like a pair of eyeglasses.

Note: There is no heather at Heather Lake.

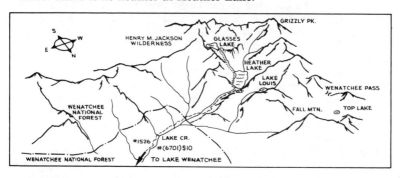

(Left) Heather Lake

52 CADY PASS— MEANDER MEADOWS LOOP

Loop trip 17½ miles; sidetrip 14 miles more
Allow 3–5 days
High point 4600 feet; sidetrip 6450 feet

Elevation gain 3000 feet, for sidetrip add 2400 feet
Hikable July through September
USGS Bench Mark Mountain, Poe Mountain, Glacier Peak

A loop hike splendid in its own right, with an opportunity for a sidetrip to White Pass along what some argue is the most beautiful segment of the entire Pacific Crest National Scenic Trail, certainly offering one of the longest meadow walks anywhere in the Cascade Range.

Drive 14.5 miles on Little Wenatchee River road No. 65 (Hike 50) to its end near Little Wenatchee Ford Campground, elevation 3000 feet.

Trail No. 1501 drops to a bridge over the Little Wenatchee River. In ¼ mile pass the Cady Ridge trail and at 3½ miles a nice camp beside Cady Creek. Follow the creek 5 miles, gaining 1700 feet (including ups and downs), to wooded and waterless 4300-foot Cady Pass. Turn right (north) on the Pacific Crest Trail, climbing 1300 feet in 2 miles to break out above timberline on the divide between Cady Creek and Pass Creek. Now the way goes around this side or that of one small knoll after another, alternating between Eastern Washington and Western Washington. Then comes a traverse along the east slope of 6368-foot Skykomish Peak. At 2½ miles from Cady Pass (8 miles from the road) is 5479-foot Lake Sally Ann, a charming little tarn amid cliff-bordered meadows, very fragile and in the past badly abused. Camping with stock is now banned, as are fires within 200 feet of the lake. Less than ½ mile farther is an intersection with the Cady Ridge trail and another camp in a broad meadow. Climb a waterfall-sparkling basin to 5680-foot Wards Pass and roam parkland atop and near the crest past Dishpan Gap to 5450-foot Sauk Pass, 5½ miles from Cady Pass (10½ miles from the road), and a junction with trail No. 1525, the return route by way of Meander Meadows. For a basecamp descend meadows to the best possible campsite or a mile farther to some super spots.

For the sidetrip continue on the Crest Trail 7 miles to 6450-foot Red Pass, more flower-covered meadows, and a spectacular view of Glacier Peak. The way goes up (1900 feet) and down (900 feet) the ridge top, totalling for the round trip 14 miles of hiking and 2400 feet of climbing— worth it.

The sidetrip begins by traversing green slopes of Kodak Peak to a saddle. (Take a few minutes to carry your camera, Kodak or other, to the 6121-foot summit.) Descend across a gorgeous alpine basin and down forest to mostly wooded Indian Pass, 5000 feet, 1½ miles from Sauk Pass. Find pleasant campsites in the pass—but usually no water except in early summer.

Climb forest and gardens around the side of Indian Head Peak to tiny Kid Pond and beyond to 5378-foot Lower White Pass, 3 miles from Sauk Pass, and a junction with the White River trail. The next 1½ miles have

Pacific Crest near Kodak Peak

the climax meadows, past Reflection Pond into flower fields culminating at 5904-foot White Pass, 4½ miles from Sauk Pass. For dramatic views of Glacier Peak and the White Chuck Glacier walk the Crest Trail west another 1½ miles to Red Pass.

Having done (or not) the sidetrip, finish the loop from Meander Meadows by following trail No. 1525 down 2 miles of flowers and another 5 miles of forest and meadow.

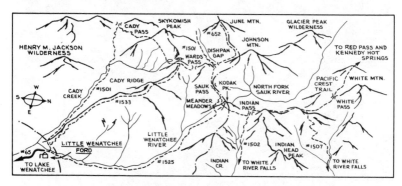

53

POE MOUNTAIN

Round trip 6 miles
Hiking time 4 hours
High point 6015 feet
Elevation gain 3000 feet

Hikable late June through
   October
One day
USGS Poe Mountain

What the map calls "Wenatchee Ridge" is unofficially known as "Poet Ridge," due to a government mapmaker of yore having named its various high points Bryant Peak, Longfellow Mountain, Poe Mountain, Irving Peak, and Whittier Peak. Discriminating students of literature call it "Poetaster Ridge" and lament the taste of government mapmakers of yore. Poe is not the highest of the lot but has so commanding a view it was once the site of a lookout cabin. The panorama includes the Little Wenatchee River valley from Meander Meadows to Soda Springs, forests of Nason Ridge, and mountains of the Cascade Crest. Views in other directions are blocked by various poets. Glacier Peak, Sloan, Monte Cristo, Hinman, and Rainier can be seen above distant ridges.

The two trails to Poe Mountain are the same length and, when ups and downs are taken into account, have nearly the same elevation gain. The better choice on a hot day would be the ridge route, reached from road No. 6504 and Irving Pass trail No. 1545, starting at an elevation of 4000 feet. The direct route from the west described here should be done early in the morning before the sun blisters the trail. Carry water; there's none along the way save dewdrops.

Mountain daisy

Drive Little Wenatchee River road No. 65 to the end, elevation 3000 feet (Hike 52).

Walk ¼ mile on Little Wenatchee River trail No. 1525 and turn right on Poe Mountain trail No. 1520. The rate of gain is about 1000 feet per mile, ideal for getting there firstest with the mostest rubber left on the lugs. Shade trees are scarce but views are plentiful, enlarging at each upward rest-step. Just below the top the way joins the ridge trail, No. 1543, for the final ¼ mile to the meadowy summit.

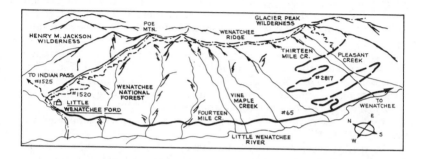

Glacier Peak and Poet Ridge from Poe Mountain

54 DIRTY FACE PEAK

Round trip 9½ miles
Hiking time 7 hours
High point 6193 feet
Elevation gain 4300 feet

Hikable mid-June through
   October
One day
USGS Wenatchee Lake

A stiff climb, cruelly hot in sunny and windless weather, to a deserted lookout site with an airy view over Lake Wenatchee and into the Glacier Peak Wilderness. The last 2½ miles are dry; carry lots of water. For hikers who don't mind a few small snowpatches, this is a fine mid-June trip.

Drive US 2 east from Stevens Pass 19 miles and turn left to Lake Wenatchee. Pass the state park road, the roads to Plain and Fish Lake, and continue to Lake Wenatchee Ranger Station. Turn right to the small campground behind the station and find the trailhead, elevation 1900 feet. (The trail can be intersected from road No. (6305)511 but through the mid-1990s this will be a heavy-hauling route, not recommended for passenger cars.)

The trail is mostly in very good shape, wide and smooth, but steep, very steep, gaining about 1000 feet a mile. (The trail sign says the peak is 4 miles but the distance is definitely 4½ miles or more.) In the first mile are several creeks. At 1½ miles intersect an abandoned logging road, follow it a scant ½ mile to its end, and pick up the trail again. Here is a good campsite in the woods, and also the last water.

The way relentlessly climbs 70 switchbacks (we counted them) to the summit ridge. At about switchback 45 the trail leaves the tall Ponderosa pine and enters alpine trees and flowers—and glorious views of the lake. From the crest it is almost ½ mile and 11 more switchbacks (for a total of 81) to the old lookout site at 6193 feet.

Enjoy views west to Nason Ridge, north up the Napeequa River to Clark Mountain, Chiwawa Ridge, and the Chiwawa valley, and east to endless hills. Below to the left is Fish Lake and, directly beneath, Lake Wenatchee. At the head of the latter, note the vast marshes and the meandering streams; at one point the White River comes within a few

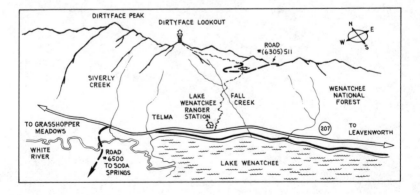

feet of the lake but snakes back another ¼ mile before entering. Ant-sized boats can be seen on the lakes, and cars on the highways.

In early July there is a rock garden of blossoming phlox. In late summer and fall the upper trail offers blueberries to sate a perhaps gigantic thirst.

Lake Wenatchee from Dirty Face Peak

55 MOUNT DAVID

Round trip 16 miles
Hiking time 10 hours
High point 7431 feet
Elevation gain 5200 feet

Hikable mid-August to October
One day or backpack
USGS Wenatchee Lake

Climb a real mountain, 7431 feet high. As with any other main-range Cascade peak of such elevation, the ascent is lengthy and strenuous. However, the cliffy summit, where climbers would otherwise rope up, has a trail blasted to a long-abandoned lookout site. (The cabin is gone, but the stone privy remains.) Enjoy panoramic views out over countless peaks and down almost a vertical mile to the river. It's best not to try the hike until August, when snow has melted from the steep and potentially dangerous gullies. The trail is dry, so carry plenty of water.

Drive from US 2 to Lake Wenatchee (Hike 54). Cross the Wenatchee River. At the bridge, check the odometer. At a big Y go left and at 9.6 miles from the bridge stay right on White River road No. 6400. At 16½ miles from the bridge reach the road-end and parking area, elevation 2300 feet.

Cross the White River on a horse bridge signed "Indian Creek Trail." On the far side enter the Glacier Peak Wilderness and turn downstream on a trail signed "Mt. David" and "Panther Creek." In 1 long mile from the bridge, where the river trail keeps left, turn right on the Mount David trail.

There is a big bundle of altitude to gain and the trail gets at it immediately. At ⅓ mile cross the last reliable stream. In 1 mile the tread is difficult to find in slide alder and vine maple of an avalanche slope. From here the trail is well graded. Relentless switchbacks grind up and up through forest to the ridge crest at 4½ miles.

The final 3½ miles follow the ups and downs of the ridge, sometimes contouring below high points, switchbacking up one gully then moving into the next. Around several cliffs the trail has been eroded away, but it is still safe. Views grow: south to Lake Wenatchee, Mt. Daniel, and Mt. Rainier and north to Clark Mountain.

Snow remains on slopes directly under the summit rocks until late August—a good reason for doing the trip no earlier. Tread is very obscure in a talus here and easily may be lost. If so, climb to the ridge and find the way where it crosses to the south side of the peak. The last few hundred feet have been blasted from cliff and improved by cement steps. Once there was even a guardrail, but it's gone now. Hikers suffering from acrophobia will be happier to settle for a conclusion somewhat short of the absolute top, 8 miles from the road.

Views are long to all horizons. Glacier Peak, 12 miles away, dominates, but careful study reveals many other mountains of the Cascade Crest; off west, above the head of Indian Creek, is Sloan Peak. Look down and down to the Indian Creek trail, crossing streamside meadows.

The only possible campsite is a flat meadow at about 5200 feet. The meadow is some 500 feet below the trail, reached by a spur descending from a short bit past the 4-mile marker.

(Top) Part of Poet Ridge from Mount David trail

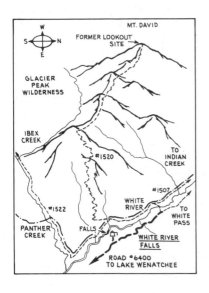

(Bottom) Trail to Mount David

56   PANTHER CREEK

Round trip 9 miles   **Hikable June to October**
Hiking time 5 hours   **One day or backpack**
High point 3600 feet   **USGS Wenatchee Lake**
Elevation gain 1600 feet in, 500
   feet out

Here's a trail with double protection: by being in the Glacier Peak Wilderness; by being so rarely maintained that windfalls and brush keep out the crowds. You may really truly be alone camped on the knoll between the gorges of Panther and Ibex Creeks. Never mind those nettle welts and barked shins.

Drive to the end of the White River road (Hike 55), elevation 2300 feet. Cross the river on the horse bridge signed "Indian Creek Trail." On the far side enter the Glacier Peak Wilderness and turn downstream on a trail signed "Mt. David" and "Panther Creek." In 1 long mile, where Mt. David trail (Hike 55) goes right, keep left. At 2 miles, having lost 300 feet, make an abrupt right turn from the White River onto Panther Creek trail No. 1522.

The trail climbs a bit, then moderates at 2½ miles (from the road) and passes a delightful creekside camp. The creek emerges from a narrow gorge, and the path must switchback up and around, sometimes steeply. At 3½ miles the brush closes in; pick your way carefully. At about 4 miles are a high point of 3600 feet, a respite from brush, and a quick little drop to a small campsite some 150 feet above the confluence of Ibex and Panther Creeks, 4½ miles from the road.

Continuing onward is likely to get you honest-to-gosh lonesome because the trail is blasted from the gorge walls and Ibex Creek must be forded until well along in summer. A miraculous feat to perform and survive. Further, not even occasional maintenance is done beyond the ford, the brush closes in, and the trail climbs the valley wall and doesn't come near Panther Creek for 2 miles.

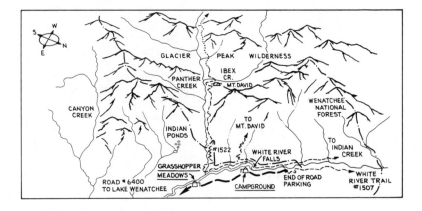

Ibex Creek

57 INDIAN CREEK—WHITE RIVER LOOP

Round trip to Indian Creek 8 miles
Hiking time 4 hours
High point 3200 feet
Elevation gain 900 feet
Hikable mid-June to October
One day or backpack
USGS Wenatchee Lake, Poe Mountain

Loop trip to Indian Creek and White River 28 miles
Allow 3–4 days
High point 5500 feet
Elevation gain 2200 feet
Hikable July to October
USGS Wenatchee Lake, Poe Mountain, Holden, Glacier Peak

Study the recipes and choose your repast: a day hike in the deep woods; an easy or lengthier overnighter; or a loop trip of 3–5 days, tacking on a sidetrip through glory gardens of the Pacific Crest Trail.

Drive the White River road to the end (Hike 55), elevation 2300 feet.

The loop, equally good in either direction, is here described clockwise. Cross the river on the horse bridge and turn upstream on Indian Creek trail No. 1502, following the White River a long 2 miles. The way then crosses Indian Creek on a bridge and tilts, gaining 800 feet in 1¾ miles. Trail and creek abruptly level off at a nice campsite, 3200 feet, 4 miles from the road. This is a dandy turnaround for a day hike or a short overnighter, though there are several other good camps the next 3 miles.

The 2 miles from the 3200-foot camp go up and down a lot, from solid ground to horse-churned mudholes, but make a net elevation gain of zero. The next 5 miles compensate by climbing moderately but steadily to Indian Pass, 5000 feet, 11 miles from the road. The camps here usually have no potable water after early summer.

Climb from parkland forest of the pass to flowers of the 5500-foot high point on the side of Indian Head Peak. Drop a bit to Lower White Pass, 5378 feet, and meet the White River trail at a scant 1½ miles from Indian Pass.

It would be a shame, having walked this far, not to romp through the gardens a little. Indeed, if you can't allow an extra day or two to sidetrip north on the Pacific Crest Trail—1 mile or 2, or the 4½ miles to Red Pass—why bother doing the loop?

The return leg descends from Lower White Pass on White River trail No. 1507. Some 4 miles from the pass a bridge over the river has been washed out. The footlogs (belly logs?) are slick. The alternative is to ford, which can be hazardous in high water, which lasts until mid-August. Consider the advantages of hiking counterclockwise, in order to confront the raging torrent on the way in, when you can readily turn back. Farther along are several long stretches of the sort of brush that thrives where avalanches forbid forests to do so. One stretch is 2 miles long. If you think you don't like it when the bushes are soaked with rain, wait until you've tried it in a blazing sun when the flies are so hungry they're eating the mosquitoes. Except for *that,* the way lies in cathedral stands of old-growth forest.

At 15 miles from Lower White Pass the loop returns to the road, for a total of 28 miles plus the side-romp north on the Cascade Crest.

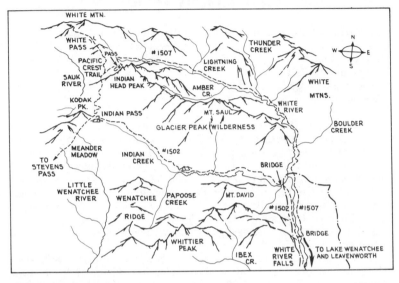

Indian Creek

58 NAPEEQUA VALLEY VIA BOULDER PASS

Round trip to Napeequa ford 26 miles
Allow 3–7 days
High point 6250 feet
Elevation gain 4250 feet in, 2000 feet out

Hikable August through September
USGS Holden and Glacier Peak

The Napeequa River has craftily designed its fabled "Shangri La" to keep people out—exiting from the valley via a cliff-walled gorge that has never had any sort of trail, entering from glaciers and precipices inaccessible except to climbers. Each of the only two reasonable accesses is over an exceedingly high pass and a wide, deep, swift river. Hikers may well climb to the top of Boulder Pass, drop to the floor of Napeequa valley—and find themselves cut off from the meadows by the Napeequa River. Then, if they get across the flood alive, they can expect to be sucked dry of blood by flies as big as the flowers and as numerous. Pretty pictures don't tell the whole story.

Drive to the end of the White River road (Hike 55), elevation 2300 feet.

Hike the White River trail #1507 4 pleasant, virtually level miles through lovely virgin forest to Boulder Pass trail No. 1562, 2470 feet. Subsequent mileages are from this junction.

The well-graded trail climbs steadily. In about 2½ miles is a crossing of Boulder Creek, hazardous in high water. At 4 miles is 5000-foot Basin Camp, under the walls of 8676-foot Clark Mountain. This is a logical and splendid spot to end the first day—and also a grand base for an extra day exploring a very faint path west to a 6150-foot saddle overlooking the White River. To find the path, cross the creek from camp to a point just under a slab of red rock on the opposite side of the valley. Even without tread the going would be fairly easy up open meadows.

From Basin Camp the trail climbs 2½ miles to 6250-foot Boulder Pass, the meadowy saddle to the immediate east of Clark Mountain. Look down into the Napeequa valley and over to Little Giant Pass (Hike 65). The hike to here, 10¾ miles from the road, makes a strenuous but richly

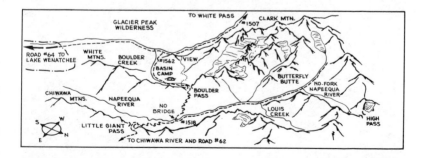

rewarding 2- to 3-day trip. You may well decide to say the heck with Shangri La and drowning.

Descend switchbacks 2¼ miles to the valley floor—and trouble—at 4340 feet. The Forest Service is unable to keep a bridge across the swift-flowing Napeequa River, which perhaps can be safely forded at this point in late August. But many summers it's never less than very risky.

If you can manage to cross, explorations are limited only by the time available. Follow the trail up the wide, green valley floor, probably the floor of an ancient lake, 5 or 6 miles; good camps are numerous. In ½ mile look to glaciers on Clark Mountain. In 2 miles pass under the falls of Louis Creek. Wander on and on, higher and higher, better and better, to trail's end in the moraines and creeks of Napeequa Basin, a deep hole half-ringed by dazzling glaciers, one of which tumbles nearly to the basin floor. Experienced off-trail travelers can find meager sidetrails into the hanging valleys of Louis Creek and North Fork Napeequa and climb to Louis Basin or 6876-foot High Pass. However, the rangers say that most people who try just get lost.

Napeequa River

Raging Creek trail's end

CHIWAWA RIVER
Unprotected area

RAGING CREEK

Round trip from trailhead 11
  miles
Hiking time 6 hours
High point 5100 feet
Elevation gain 2700 feet in, 1100
  feet out

Hikable late June through
  October
One day or backpack
USGS Lake Wenatchee

The trail is rugged—seldom used, less often maintained—the kind of trail used by hikers who are gluttons for punishment. But the views down to the Chiwawa valley and out to the Glacier Peak Wilderness are all the better for the misery. Experienced off-trail hikers will so savor the spice they'll want to basecamp and explore.

Drive US 2 east from Stevens Pass and turn north toward Lake Wenatchee. A short distance past the Wenatchee River bridge keep right at a Y, go 1.5 miles on county road No. 22, and turn left on Chiwawa River road No. 62 for 2.4 miles. Turn left on road No. 6300, and at 5.8 miles from the Chiwawa River road, go right on road No. 6306. At 6.3 miles keep left at a major (unmarked) junction. At 9.5 miles from the Chiwawa River road reach the Raging Creek trailhead, elevation 2700 feet. From here the road is gated against public use from October 1 to July 1 for wildlife protection. The Forest Service wishes you would walk the whole trail because logging will be heavy indefinitely and parking may be unsafe. However, if the gate is open you may prefer to drive exactly 2 miles to an unmarked intersection with the trail. Look carefully, just where the road reaches a forested saddle. The trail is back in the woods about a hundred feet, elevation 3500 feet. There is no room to park here, so drive on another ¼ mile and walk back. The logging road does not show on Forest Service maps; neither road nor trail is on the USGS map.

Trail No. 1541 survives its neglect quite nicely. The huckleberry bushes grow to an ideal height for a hiker to be able to browse the fruit, in season, using no hands. At 2 miles from the saddle the way crosses a 5000-foot high point, drops steeply 600 feet, crosses a tributary of Raging Creek and resumes climbing. A short bit beyond the stream is a good camp.

The trail makes an ascending traverse on the side of a steep ridge, discouraging the walker with three descents of a hundred feet or more. At 5 miles on a big-view shoulder, 5100 feet, is a great turnaround for day-hikers. There are views of 6930-foot Crook Mountain and a rocky summit across the deep Raging Creek valley. Campers will drop 200 feet to several small tarns, another tributary of Raging Creek, and campsites ¼ mile upstream.

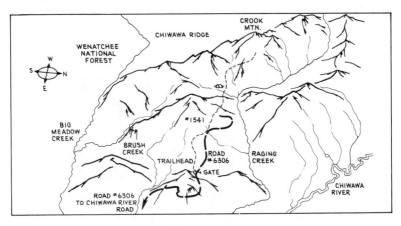

60 BASALT RIDGE—GARLAND PEAK

Round trip 9 miles
Allow 2 days
High point 6500 feet
Elevation gain 2600 feet in, 500
feet out

Hikable July to October
USGS Lucerne and Plain

The trail along Basalt Ridge to the Garland Peak area of the Entiat Mountains gives views across Rock Creek to Old Gib Mountain and beyond to the ice-gleaming spires of Clark Mountain and Glacier Peak. There are four ways to reach Basalt Ridge: the hard way, Minnow Creek; over the top of Basalt Peak (Hike 61); the steep 4 miles up Rock Creek (Hike 63); and the terribly steep (but short, only 1¼ miles) access described here.

Drive the Chiwawa River road (Hike 59) 9.4 miles from county road No. 22 and turn right on road No. 6210 for 5.7 miles to trail No. 1530, elevation 3900 feet.

The trail starts steep, relents briefly, and reverts to type, henceforth showing little mercy. The amazing thing is that the Forest Service permits horses. (Motorcycles are banned.) As a general rule of thumb, a single horse damages a trail as much as 20 hikers; on a steep trail like this, though, the proportion must be one horse to 50 or 100 hikers.

In 1¼ miles the trail climbs 1200 feet to a 5700-foot saddle and an unsigned junction with Basalt Ridge trail No. 1515. Several hundred feet uphill to the left is the signed junction with the access trail from Rock Creek. Go right along the saddle, losing about 50 feet, then climbing a moderately steep, rocky slope, emerging from trees to buckbrush meadows. These give way to meadows that are almost all stones, very few plants.

At about 3 miles from the road the way attains a high point, 6500 feet, with views big enough to satisfy the day-hiker—who by now will have been laboring 2 or 3 or 4 hours. Overnighters will continue, losing about

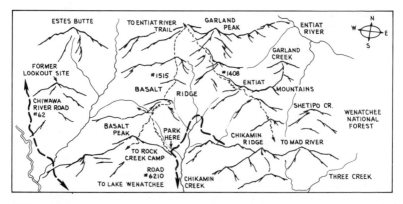

Basalt Ridge trail

200 feet, gaining them back, and contouring the slopes of a knob to a 6500-foot saddle at the edge of a huge pumice field (deposited by Glacier Peak 12,000 years ago). Descend a way trail 500 feet to campsites—and the only water of the trip—below Garland Peak.

For explorations, continue on the Basalt Ridge trail to the Garland Peak trail (Hike 84) and proceed north or south.

61   BASALT PEAK

Round trip 8 miles
Hiking time 6 hours
High point 6004 feet
Elevation gain 3500 feet

Hikable June through October
One day
USGS Wenatchee Lake and Plain

Though the summit of Basalt Peak is covered with trees, a few feet away is a naked knoll with views up the length of Rock Creek, down to the logging roads of Chikamin Creek, and across the valley to Garland Peak, Devils Smokestack, Fifth of July Mountain, and a row of nameless summits in the Entiat Mountains. There are four ways (all steep) to the top: Minnow Creek, Basalt Ridge (Hike 60), Rock Creek (Hike 63), and the Basalt Peak trail described here.

Drive the Chiwawa River road (Hike 59) 12.8 miles from county road No. 22 to the site of the old guard station, a small campsite, and Basalt Peak trail, signed "Basalt Ridge," elevation 2474 feet.

Starting with a steep 1¼ miles (an hour's steady pounding for a swift walker, thrice that for a gasping plodder), the trail flattens some to an intersection, 1½ miles, 4600 feet, with the Minnow Creek trail from the Chikamin Creek road. The way resumes the ascent, switchbacking up the west slope of Basalt Peak to within a dozen feet of the wooded summit, 6004 feet, then dipping to the view knoll, a great finish.

The trail drops 900 more feet in 1 mile to the junction of trail No. 1530 (Hike 60), then climbs to the Garland Peak trail (Hike 84). If Garland Peak is the destination, this definitely is the hard way.

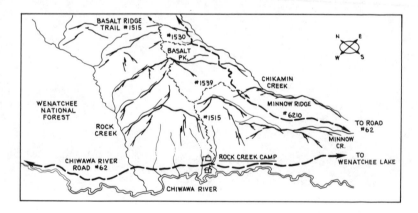

View from Basalt Peak after September snowstorm

SCHAEFER LAKE

Round trip 10 miles
Hiking time 6 hours
High point 5131 feet
Elevation gain 2700 feet

Hikable June through October
One day or backpack
USGS Wenatchee Lake

A forest trail leads to a sparkling lake amid rocky ridges. First, however, a person must get to the trail, which lies on the far side of the Chiwawa River, only safe to wade in late summer. So, is the good old logjam still in place? Thereby hangs the decision, to go or not to go.

Drive the Chiwawa River road (Hike 59) 14 miles from county road No. 22 to .2 mile upstream from Rock Creek Guard Station and Schaefer Lake trail No. 1519, elevation 2474 feet.

The trail drops to the river and—one hopes—the logjam. On the far side it pokes along the Chiwawa valley floor for a magnificent mile of spruce and cedar forest. It then runs up against the valley wall and makes a long uphill traverse in the woods, with a couple of short switchbacks and occasional glimpses to snowy summits of Red Mountain, Dumbell, and Seven-Fingered Jack. At about 2½ miles the way rounds the corner into the valley of Schaefer Creek, passing a possible camp just short of 3 miles and at 3½ miles crossing the creek on a sturdy bridge, 4100 feet.

The trail now does business, climbing 1000 feet in 1¼ miles (at 4½ miles is the boundary of Glacier Peak Wilderness). The ascent slackens, passing Lower Schaefer Lake, a shallow pond, and reaching Upper Schaefer Lake at 5 miles, 5131 feet.

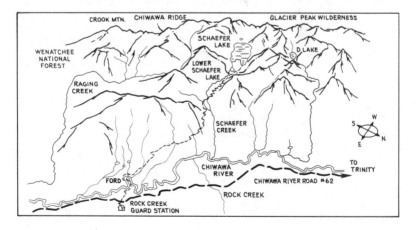

Schaefer Lake

63 ROCK CREEK

Round trip 14 miles
Allow 2 days
High point 4300 feet
Elevation gain 1800 feet

Hikable mid-June to October
USGS Holden and Wenatchee
Lake

Looking for a spot just like Spider Meadow, except with the flowers outnumbering the hikers? This forest trail leads to campsites at the edge of Rock Creek Meadow, not as big as the Spider but equally beautiful and generally deserted.

Drive the Chiwawa River road (Hike 59) 14.5 miles from county road No. 22. Just before the Rock Creek bridge find Rock Creek trail No. 1509, on the right side of the road, elevation 2515 feet.

Built wide and hard to let motorcyclists go fast enough to get bugs in their teeth, the trail climbs gently the first mile, steepens a bit the second mile, and at 2¼ miles, 3400 feet, comes to a junction. The right fork climbs to the Basalt Ridge trail (Hike 60); keep straight ahead, left. The trail, at this point some 400–500 feet above Rock Creek, contours (with ups and downs) the next 1¾ miles, letting the river catch up to the trail level.

At 4½ miles the route enters the Glacier Peak Wilderness, drops a bit, and enters a magnificent forest of big trees. Just beyond the 5-mile marker is a choice little campsite near the stream. At about 5½ miles, where the original water-grade trail tread slid out years ago, is a miserable detour over a cliff.

Starting with the detour, the trail is no more Mr. Nice Guy, becoming rough and steep. Occasional windows open in the forest to Devils Smokestack, Fifth of July Mountain, and nameless peaks of the Entiat Mountains. At 6¼ miles is a crossing—difficult until late summer—of Rock Creek. At 7 miles the way passes through the promised meadow to excellent campsites at the second crossing of the creek, 4300 feet.

For easy explorations from a basecamp here, continue upstream to

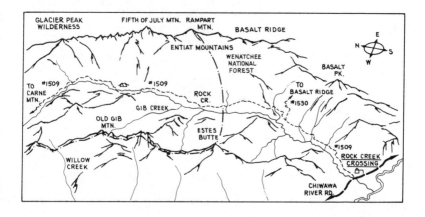

more meadows or hike 5 more miles (gaining 2700 feet) to the lookout site on Carne Mountain (Hike 69). Consider a loop trip via Carne Mountain and Estes Butte (Hike 64); in addition to the above, add 10 miles, for a loop total of 22 miles, elevation gain of about 5000 feet.

Rock Creek trail

Face of Estes Butte

CHIWAWA RIVER
Unprotected area

ESTES BUTTE

Round trip 5 miles
Hiking time 4 hours
High point 5402 feet
Elevation gain 2900 feet

Hikable June to October
One day
USGS Wenatchee Lake

A supersteep trail climbs to a former lookout site on a 5402-foot bump on the ridge leading to Estes Butte. Do the hike in midsummer when the forest floor is blooming with sidebells pyrola and pipsissewa or on a crisp fall day when the sun cheers but not overheats. Motorcycles and horses soon would destroy the tread, so wheels are banned and hooves discouraged, making the trail virtually hiker-only.

Drive the Chiwawa River road (Hike 59) 14.7 miles from county road No. 22. Just beyond Rock Creek bridge turn right on a rough track several hundred feet to a small campground and Estes Butte trail No. 1527 (perhaps unsigned), elevation 2525 feet.

The trail parallels Rock Creek a short, level way to join a rough old mining road. Turn right on the jeep road and follow it steeply upward. Where it flattens at the top of the steep stretch, find the foot trail going even more steeply up into woods to the right. The path gains between 1000 and 1200 feet per mile, an ideal grade for a hiker. The slow pace gives plenty of time to look down to the pyrola and pipsissewa. In the first mile there are a few looks out through chinks in the green wall to views down the valley, and in the second mile some windows on green meadows of the Entiat Mountains to the east.

At 2½ miles is the old lookout site, 5402 feet (according to the USGS benchmark). The building was atop a tower with an all-points view over the tree tops. Only the concrete foundation remains, but by moving about and looking between trees the same view can be assembled from the pieces. Day-trippers should eat their cookies here and go home.

The trail continues another 12 miles, with major ups and downs, over the tippy-top of Estes Butte, into the Glacier Peak Wilderness, around the side of Old Gib Mountain, to Carne Mountain (Hike 69), gaining 2500 feet on the way. The route is dangerous before the snow melts and bone-dry afterward.

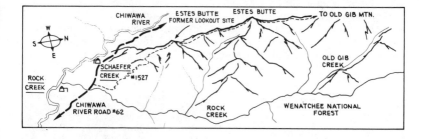

65 NAPEEQUA VALLEY VIA LITTLE GIANT PASS

Round trip to the pass 9½ miles
Hiking time 9 hours
High point 6409 feet
Elevation gain 4200 feet in, 300 feet out

Hikable early August through September
One day or backpack
USGS Holden

Climb to the famous view of the fabled Napeequa valley. Look down on the silvery river meandering through green meadows of the old lakebed. See the gleaming ice on Clark Mountain and Tenpeak, glimpse a piece of Glacier Peak. But you gotta really want it. Strong mountaineers turn pale at memories of Little Giant in sunshine and flytime. However, though more grueling than the Boulder Pass entry (Hike 58), the trail is 5 miles shorter and has no fearsome ford of the Napeequa to face. Ah, but it may have a fearsome ford of the Chiwawa River. But that's at the very beginning, so you get the bad news in time to choose another destination should the logjam be missing and the flood be boiling halfway up your Kelty.

Drive the Chiwawa River road about 19 miles from county road No. 22. Spot a barricaded sideroad left, signed "Bridge Out." Park here, elevation 2600 feet.

Longingly inspect remains of the bridge taken out by a flood in 1972. Look around for a logjam. Finding none, try the wade, if you are fairly sure you can survive it, and if you do, follow abandoned roads through abandoned Maple Creek Campground toward the mountainside, and pretty soon pick up the trail. The old straight-up sheep driveway of evil reputation has been partly replaced (and the sheep are long gone from here, too) by a trail that was nicely engineered, if steep, but is deteriorating rapidly from lack of maintenance. The way climbs the valley of

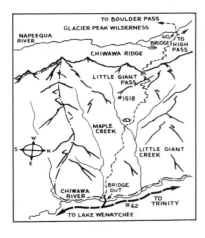

Glacier lily

Napeequa River from Little Giant Pass

Maple Creek in pretty pine forest, crosses a saddle, and drops to South Fork Little Giant Creek at about 2½ miles from the river, 4000 feet. Campsites are on both sides.

Now the way steepens and at 3 miles half-scrambles up a broad rib of bare schist that splits the valley in two and on a sunny day will fry your boots. But in ⅓ mile creeks begin. So do camps that get progressively better, the last on a scenic meadow knoll at 4 miles. A lovely ascent in greenery and marmots leads to the 6409-foot pass, 4⅔ miles from the river.

Better views can be obtained by scrambling up the knobs on either side of the pass, which in addition to being a sensational grandstand is a glory of flowers.

The trail down to the Napeequa is poorly maintained if at all, yet suffices for hikers—but not for horses or sheep, and bleached bones prove it. Watch your step—at spots a misstep could add you to the casualty list. The distance to the 4200-foot valley floor is 2 miles, and if the views don't have you raving, the blossoms will. Or, in season, the flies. The trail proceeds upvalley 1⅓ miles to the site of the bridge that is gone and the ford that remains to cross the river to the Boulder Pass trail (Hike 58). The best camps hereabouts are on gravel bars—but watch out for sudden high water on hot afternoons.

66 BUCK CREEK PASS— HIGH PASS

Round trip 19 miles
Allow 2–3 days
High point 6000 feet

Elevation gain 3200 feet
Hikable July through October
USGS Holden

In a mountain range full to overflowing with "unique places," two things have given Buck Creek Pass fame: an unusual richness of flower gardens rising from creek bottoms to high summits, and the exceptional view of the grandest ice streams of Glacier Peak, seen across the broad, forested valley of the Suiattle River. The trail lends itself to a variety of trips short and long: a day's walk as far as time allows, a weekend at the pass, or a week of explorations.

Drive the Chiwawa River road (Hike 59) about 24 miles from county road No. 22 to the end at Phelps Creek, elevation 2772 feet, next to the old mining town of Trinity.

Triad Lake and Clark Mountain from High Pass trail

Walk across the Phelps Creek bridge into Trinity and follow trail signs (no loitering or exploring on this private land) past the buildings and over the valley floor until the old roads become trail. At ¾ mile a sign announces entry into the Glacier Peak Wilderness. A nice creek runs in forest shade. The abandoned road climbs moderately to a junction at 1½ miles. The road leads straight ahead toward mining claims on Red Mountain (Hike 67); the trail turns left.

Tread goes up and down within sound of the Chiwawa River. At 2¾ miles cross the "river" (now just a fast-moving creek) and enter the valley of Buck Creek. Just beyond the bridge is a large campsite.

The trail climbs a valley step, levels out, and passes a forest camp in a patch of grass, switchbacks up another glacier-gouged step, and emerges from trees to traverse a wide avalanche meadow at 5 miles, 4300 feet. This is a good turnaround for a day hike, offering a view of the cliffs and hanging glaciers on the north wall of 8573-foot Buck Mountain.

There are many small campsites along the way. Most notable are those at 7 miles, 4500 feet, across Buck Creek on a green meadow, and another ¼ mile farther up the trail in the woods. From this point the trail starts a series of long switchbacks, climbing on a 10-percent grade to a 6000-foot high point overlooking Buck Creek Pass, 9½ miles. For camping, drop about 200 feet into the pass; the area is mobbed on weekends.

Explorations? Enough for a magnificent week.

Start with an evening wander to Flower Dome to watch Suiattle forests darken into night while the snows of Glacier Peak glow pink.

For a spectacular sunrise, carry your sleeping bag to the top of Liberty Cap.

Try an interesting sheepherders' track. Walk the main trail back toward Trinity about ½ mile from the pass to a large basin with several streams. A few feet before emerging from forest into basin meadows, go left on an unmarked way trail that traverses flower gardens below Helmet Butte and Fortress Mountain, past delightful campsites, disappearing in some 2 miles at 6100 feet.

Don't miss the dead-end trail toward (not to) High Pass. Find it on the south side of Buck Creek Pass and ascend around Liberty Cap and as far as the way is not covered with dangerously steep snow. The end, 3 miles from Buck Creek Pass, is in a 7200-foot saddle overlooking the wintry basin of Triad Lake. Getting from trail's end to High Pass is a task for climbers.

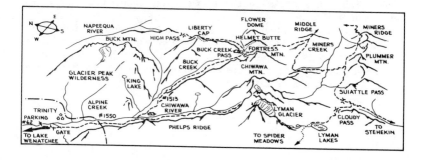

67   RED MOUNTAIN

Round trip 16½ miles
Allow 2 days
High point 6900 feet
Elevation gain 4100 feet

Hikable mid-July through
September
USGS Holden

Mining operations, mainly in the 1920s and 30s but with some messing around in the 1950s, have bruised and ripped and battered the fragile subalpine terrain. The old trail has been replaced by an ugly, rutted prospectors' road. Not for centuries will nature repair the damage. Keep it in mind as an object lesson next time you hear defenders of the antique Mining Laws bray about "free enterprise." Not all is lost, however. The surviving meadows are beautiful, and the views of the Upper Chiwawa River basin are splendid.

Drive the Chiwawa River road (Hike 59) about 24 miles to the end at Phelps Creek, elevation 2772 feet.

Walk across the Phelps Creek bridge into Trinity and follow trail signs (no loitering or exploring on this private land) past buildings of the old Red Mountain mine and mill. At ¾ mile enter Glacier Peak Wilderness. Trust the signs to lead through the maze of old roads up the Chiwawa River 1½ miles to where Buck Creek Pass trail No. 1513 (Hike 66) branches left. Continue on the road—officially, Chiwawa River trail No. 1550—as it steadily ascends the valley on the flanks of Phelps Ridge, the way muddy from tromping by many hooves.

At 4¾ miles pass the Massie Lake route turnoff, 4400 feet. At 5¾ miles, 4900 feet, the route splits. The left fork is Chiwawa Basin trail No. 1550A, which is brushed out 1 mile farther into the basin, offering several appealing campsites.

In days past the prospectors had a loop through the basin that rejoined the other fork high on Red Mountain.

Trail No. 1550, the right fork, sticks with the road, climbing through avalanche brush, then timber, in a series of long switchbacks. At the top of the last one is a fine campsite (if not recently used by horses) at the edge of a large green basin below the brightly colored rock slopes of Red Mountain. At this point the unmaintained, difficult-to-find, and harder-to-stay-on Phelps Ridge trail No. 1514 takes off across meadows, climbs to a 6800-foot pass, and descends the far side of the ridge to a ford of Phelps Creek and a junction with trail No. 1511, reached about 1½ miles below Spider Meadow.

The road-trail now cuts a broad scar across the meadows of Red Mountain, traversing to the lower slopes of Chiwawa Mountain. The end is on a talus where trails branch every which way to little holes in the ground. For excellent alpine camping, descend the rubble to open benches amid the all-around splash of waterfalls.

Camping on Red Mountain

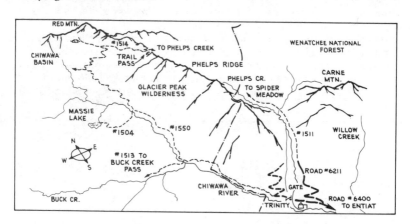

68 SPIDER MEADOW

Round trip to upper Spider Meadow 12½ miles
Hiking time 8 hours
High point 5100 feet
Elevation gain 1700 feet

Hikable mid-July through October
One day or backpack
USGS Holden

A glorious valley-bottom meadow in a seeming cul-de-sac amid rugged peaks. Yet the trail ingeniously breaks through the cliffs and climbs to a little "glacier" and a grand overlook of Lyman Basin and summits of the Cascade Crest. For hikers trained in use of the ice ax this can be merely the beginning of a long and classic loop trip.

Drive the Chiwawa River road (Hike 59) about 22 miles from county road No. 22 and turn right on No. 6211, the Phelps Creek road. Go 2 miles to a gate and the trailhead, elevation 3500 feet.

The walk begins past the gate on the road, which is still used by miners almost to the wilderness boundary.

The gentle grade goes up and down in forest, passing the Carne Mountain trail in ¼ mile, Box Creek in 1 mile, Chipmunk Creek in 1¾ miles, and the Glacier Peak Wilderness boundary in 2⅔ miles. At 3½ miles, 4175 feet, are the crossing of Leroy Creek, the junction with Leroy Creek trail, a campsite, and the end of the old road.

The way continues through forest interspersed with flower gardens. At 5¼ miles, 4700 feet, is the spectacular opening-out into Spider Meadow; here are good camps. Red Mountain shows its cliffs and snows; the views include other walls enclosing Phelps headwaters—no way can be seen to escape the valley, an apparent dead-end. A mile of flower-walking leads to the crossing of Phelps Creek, 6¼ miles, 5000 feet. A bit beyond are ruins of Ed Linston's cabin. Find good camps here, too. Hikers with only a day or a weekend may turn back, contented.

But there is much more, including more good camps. Follow the trail through the meadow, boulder-hop Phelps Creek, and proceed upward. At 6½ miles, 5300 feet, is a junction. The right fork follows Phelps Creek to more meadows and the end of the valley under Dumbell Mountain.

The left fork is a steep, hot, and very dry miners' trail climbing 1100

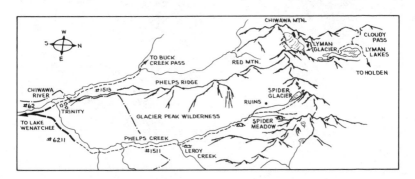

feet to the lower end of Spider Glacier at 6400 feet. Here are several tiny but spectacular campsites. There's no wood but lots of water and lots of views downvalley to Spider Meadow, Mt. Maude, and Seven-Fingered Jack.

Immediately above is the narrow snowfield of Spider Glacier. In a short mile, either up the snow-filled gully or along the easy and scenic rock spur to the east, is 7100-foot Spider Pass. Look down to the Lyman Glacier, the ice-devastated upper Lyman Basin, and the greenery of the lower basin.

An old trail ascends ¼ mile from the pass to a mine tunnel. One must marvel at the dogged energy of Ed Linston, who hauled machinery and supplies to so airy a spot. After being badly injured by a dynamite explosion in the mine, he was helped down the mountain by his brother. He recovered to spend many more years roaming the Cascades, passing away in 1969 at the age of 82.

Spider Meadow

69   CARNE MOUNTAIN

Round trip 7 miles
Hiking time 7 hours
High point 7085 feet
Elevation gain 3585 feet

Hikable July through October
One day or backpack
USGS Holden

Loll around an enchanting basin, enjoying the hideaway seclusion among soaring peaks. Then climb to the summit of Carne Mountain and gaze to the dark summit of mighty Mt. Maude, empress of the Entiat Mountains, and around to Spider Meadow, Red Mountain, Glacier Peak, Ten Peak Mountain, and Mt. Rainier.

Drive the Chiwawa River and Phelps Creek roads (Hike 68) to Phelps Creek trail No. 1511, elevation 3500 feet.

Begin with a scant ¼ mile on the Phelps Creek trail, then turn uphill on Carne Mountain trail No. 1508, ascending a very steep slope through open forest. After the first mile there are occasional windows west to the impressive massif of Chiwawa Ridge. Forest eventually is left below, broad vistas commence. At 2½ miles is a marginal campsite, water supplied by the creek from Carne Basin, which is entered at 3 miles. The greenery of the 6100-foot floor is boxed in by rocky ridges from Carne Mountain. Camps are plentiful in the lovely alpine meadows, though some are horsey and all, in season, are quite buggy. The basin boasts one of the world's largest subalpine larches, which reminds us that in October the forests hereabout turn golden and the bugs have all bugged out to California for the winter.

The trail disappears in the meadow, reappears as the ascent resumes on the far side. At 3½ miles the Carne Mountain trail splits in two. The right fork, Old Gib trail No. 1509, climbs to a nearby saddle, 6500 feet with views of the north face of Old Gib Mountain, then heads south to Estes Butte (Hike 64) and the Chiwawa River road, reached at Rock Creek.

Take the left fork, Rock Creek trail No. 1511, passing at the first switchback a steep but inviting sidetrail to the former site of a fire

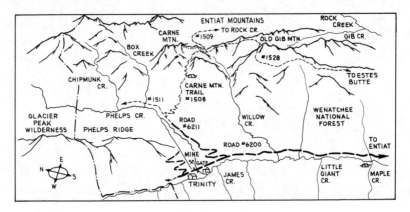

Mount Maude from Carne Mountain

lookout atop Peak 6991. Continue on the full ¾ mile to a delightful open saddle with a view of Rock Creek valley, Entiat Mountains, and the awesome massif of Mt. Maude.

The peak-grabbers should go left (north) and follow the footsteps of other peak-grabbers to 7085-foot summit of Carne Mountain. The view is not really better at the top, it just seems that way.

Alpine meadow on Miners Ridge

CHIWAWA RIVER
Unprotected area

MINERS RIDGE

Round trip 4½ miles
Hiking time 2½ hours
High point 5750 feet
Elevation gain 900 feet

Hikable late June through
   October
One day
USGS Sugarloaf Peak

In early June the meadows are brilliant with acres and acres of red paintbrush, and always there are views of the Stuart Range, Lake Wenatchee, and Glacier Peak. The Forest Service promotes the trail for motorcycles, but it's so short that a rider can do the whole thing in a few minutes, hardly worth driving the tortuous road to the trailhead. A hiker, however, moving at a sedate pace and pausing to sniff the wildflowers, can get a half-day of pleasure from the same trail. ("To make the world larger, go slower.")

With transportation arranged, this can be a one-way hike, starting from either end. It is described here from the north end because the distance is slightly less to the recommended turnaround for those not hiking on through.

The trailhead can be reached by driving road No. 5200 south 3.4 rough miles from Maverick Saddle (Hike 72). Alternately, drive highway No. 209, signed "Plain," from Leavenworth 2 miles, turn right on the county road signed "Eagle Creek Ranch," which becomes road No. 7520. At 11.5 miles from the highway go left on road No. 5200. At 15.8 miles pass the Sugarloaf Lookout road and at 17 miles reach the south Miners Ridge trailhead, elevation 5400 feet. At 19 miles is the north trailhead, trail No. 1411, elevation 4850 feet.

The trail from the north end starts by dropping 50 feet to cross Miners Creek and climbing steeply ½ mile. The tread is so badly rutted by the combination of wheels and water that hikers sometimes must walk beside it. The angle moderates before a junction at 1 mile with the abandoned Harder Two trail. From here the trip is unalloyed joy, along a ridge crest in forest with a groundcover of lupine, the perfume so rich in July a hiker may swoon into dreams of houris and honeydew, then sky-open meadows dotted with shrubby little trees. Continue south until just beyond 2 miles, where the trail descends into forest.

Unless doing the one-way plan, turn back; for more flowers and views, follow a faint game trace to the 5750-foot high point of Miners Ridge.

If continuing on, at 2¾ miles pass the abandoned Harder One trail. At 3 miles, atop a 5632-foot high point with limited views, pass the Hornet Ridge trail. At 4½ miles reach road No. 5200 at the south trailhead.

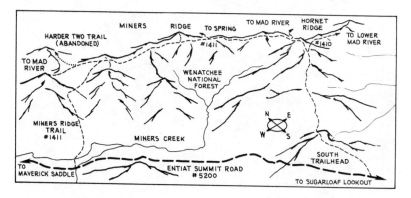

71 ALDER CREEK—MAD LAKE

Round trip 17 miles
Hiking time 8 hours
High point 6200 feet
Elevation gain 2200 feet in, 400 feet out

Hikable late June to mid-October
One day or backpack
USGS Plain

Of the various ways to the famous meadows of Mad River country, this is among the most strenuous. Moreover, unlike the Mad River route (Hike 72), no campsite with water is to be found short of Mad Lake. How-

Glacier Peak and Alder Creek trail

ever, sweat and thirst are forgotten on a glory of a ridge walk, in views from Glacier Peak to Mt. Stuart. The trail has recently been reconstructed for motorcycles, including the installation of concrete blocks to bank the corners. As soon as the motorcycles and concrete blocks are removed (keep the faith, write letters), the trail will make an excellent path for hikers and horses only.

If transportation can be arranged, the ridge run is an excellent exit for a one-way walk from the usual access to Mad Lake via Maverick Saddle and the Mad River. However, even if taken for an in-out round trip, this route has one major advantage (other than the views): though the road to Alder Ridge trailhead is long and dusty, it generally is in much better shape than that to Maverick Saddle.

From county road No. 22, between Lake Wenatchee and Plain, drive to the east side of the Chiwawa River bridge, go north on road No. 6100 for 1.6 miles and turn right on road No. 6101, signed "Maverick Saddle." In 2.3 miles turn left on road No. 6104 for 8.2 miles to Alder Ridge trail No. 1523, elevation 4000 feet.

The trail begins in forest, featuring a scattering of big, beautiful, old Ponderosa pine and Douglas fir. At 3½ miles holes begin in the greenery, permitting looks out to far country; at 4 miles, 5800 feet, a rock outcrop gives a view of Glacier Peak. The next 2 miles the way runs the ridge, often down but more often up, alternating between forest and meadow. From a 6200-foot high point the way descends 400 feet in 1 mile to a crossing of Mad River (here, a mere little creek) and joins Mad River trail No. 1409 just ½ mile south of Mad Lake.

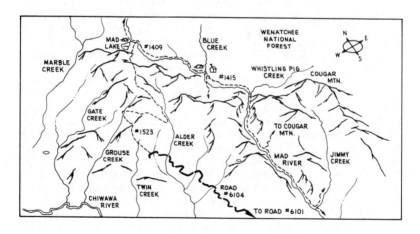

72 MAD RIVER—BLUE CREEK CAMPGROUND—MAD LAKE

**Round trip to Blue Creek
 Campground 12 miles
Allow 2 days
High point 5400 feet
Elevation gain 1200 feet
Hikable July to mid-October
USGS Chikamin Creek and Silver
 Falls**

**Round trip from Maverick Saddle
 to Mad Lake 16 miles
Allow 2 days
High point 5700 feet
Elevation gain 1550 feet**

The Mad River country of the Entiat Mountains offers miles and miles of easy, pleasant, family-style roaming. Trails follow noisy creeks through picturesque glades, trails cross broad meadows of brilliant flowers, trails round shores of little lakes, and trails climb mountains. This and the other hikes described here offer a wealth of fun and peace for a weekend or for a week-long vacation to be enjoyed by old and very young alike. Unfortunately, the Forest Service has dedicated the trails to motorcycles and is reconstructing and relocating them to permit higher (noisier) speeds, deliberately converting trails to motorcycle expressways. The proposed Mad River Hiking Area, restricting travel to hikers and horses, will correct the situation. Write letters to your congressman and senators with copies to the Forest Service.

From county road No. 22 at the Chiwawa River bridge (Hike 59) drive north on road No. 6100 for 1.6 miles and turn right on road No. 6101, signed "Maverick Saddle." At 7.3 miles from the bridge, after a final steep and narrow 2 miles only a 4x4 could love, is Maverick Saddle. An even rougher road, probably best walked, leads .3 mile to the start of Mad River trail No. 1409, elevation 4250 feet.

The trail goes downriver 15 miles to Pine Flat on the Entiat River. It also goes upriver, your way to go. In 1 mile cross a bridge over the Mad River—at this point really just a pretty creek. At 1½ miles is Jimmy Creek trail, first of three routes to the summit of 6719-foot Cougar Mountain (Hike 74). At 3 miles is an intersection with a trail that goes right to the top of Cougar, left to Lost Lake (Hike 73). At 4 miles cross Mad River on a log and at 4½ miles recross near a junction with Tyee Ridge trail No. 1415, the third way up Cougar. At 5 miles is a broad meadow and at 5½ miles, 5400 feet, Blue Creek Campground, a splendid spot for the family to spread out gear in the open campground or a secluded nook and set out on ramblings. The guard station located here is the last remains of the Mad River Dude Ranch, a popular resort in the late 1920s. The cookhouse stood near the present campground. The blacksmith shop and other buildings were scattered about.

The first ramble, of course, is to continue on the Mad River trail through a series of meadows. At 2 miles from Blue Creek Campground (8 miles from the road) go left on a scant ¼-mile trail to Mad Lake, 5700 feet. On the west shore are excellent camps with water from the inlet stream. As is true of most lakes hereabouts, this one is so silted-in that

Early morning at Mad Lake

the bottom is too mucky for wading. However, the inlet stream has deposited enough sand to make a semi-solid beach suitable for cooling the feet.

A mandatory sidetrip is the romp through glorious views along the last 2 miles of the Alder Ridge trail (Hike 71).

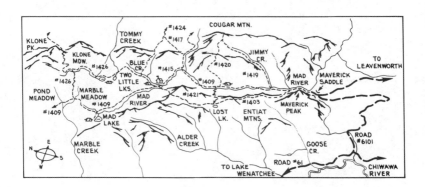

73 HI YU—LOST LAKE LOOP

Loop trip 14½ miles
Hiking time 7 hours
High point 5900 feet
Elevation gain 2100 feet

Hikable July to October
One day or backpack
USGS Silver Falls, Chikamin
Creek, Sugarloaf Peak

All the numerous opportunities on this trail are stimulating. None is easy because in spots the way is extremely steep and badly eroded by wheels, too rough to be recommended for hikers laboring under heavy packs. However, a 3-hour saunter to a viewpoint overlooking Lake Wenatchee and the Stuart Range shouldn't be too painful, not with the bonus, in season, of flowers. A 9-mile, all-day loop hike has more views and throws in Lost Lake for good measure. An excellent way to enjoy the trail is to use it as an alternate return to the road from Blue Creek Campground.

Drive to Maverick Saddle (Hike 72), elevation 4250 feet.

Hike Mad River trail No. 1409 for 1 mile and go left on Hi Yu trail No. 1403. Ascend to the ridge crest at 4900 feet, turn right and continue a steady climb through small meadows, in midsummer a solid blue with lupine bloom. Very steep, wheel-gouged, and water-gullied stretches elicit a few groans, mixed with gasps of delight at the brilliance of scarlet gilia. A 5665-foot high point, about 3 miles from the road, is the turnaround for that 3-hour hike.

The loop route drops steeply, climbs steeply, drops again, climbs again, to Lost Lake, 5600 feet, lost in tall subalpine trees, 4½ miles from the road. The camps here are supplied with water solely by the shallow lake. When thirsty, drink hot tea.

At the far end of the lake is a junction. For the short (all-day) loop, take trail No. 1421, dropping in 1½ miles to the Mad River trail, reached at 3 miles from the road, for a total of 9 miles.

For the backpack loop go left, climbing to a 5900-foot high point and dropping to Blue Creek Meadow Campground, 5400 feet, 2½ miles from Lost Lake. Finish the 14½-mile loop with 6 miles downstream on the Mad River trail to the road.

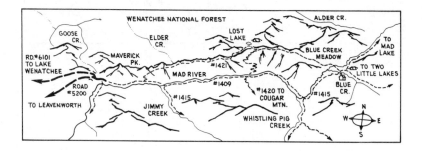

Hi Yu trail

74 COUGAR MOUNTAIN

Round trip 11 miles
Hiking time 6 hours
High point 6701 feet
Elevation gain 2500 feet

Hikable mid-June through
  October
One day
USGS Silver Falls and Sugarloaf
  Peak

It's a stiff climb to the top of Cougar, but the panoramas from the old lookout site extend from Mt. Rainier to Glacier Peak. The rock gardens near the summit also are worth the effort, especially when the snow has just melted away in late June or early July and the very stones seem to burst into bloom. The trip can be done as a sortie from a backpack base at Blue Creek Campground (Hike 72) or, as described here, a 1-day jaunt from Maverick Saddle trailhead.

Drive to Maverick Saddle (Hike 72), elevation 4250 feet.

Start out with 1½ miles on Mad River trail No. 1409. A short bit past the Mad River crossing, turn right on Jimmy Creek trail No. 1419, gaining 1400 feet in 2½ miles to a junction with abandoned trail No. 1420. Keep right for ½ mile, contouring past a junction with Cougar Ridge trail No. 1418, to a junction with trail No. 1415. Turn left, climbing 500 feet, and attain the sky-surrounded summit, 6701 feet, at 5½ miles from the road.

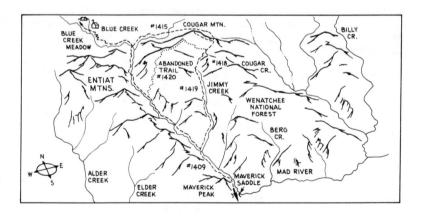

Glacier Peak from Cougar Mountain

75   TWO LITTLE LAKES

**Round trip from Blue Creek
  Campground 4 miles (from
  Maverick Saddle 16 miles)
Hiking time 3 hours
High point 5700 feet
Elevation gain 500 feet in, 200 feet
  out**

**Hikable July to mid-October
One day
USGS Chickamin Creek and
  Silver Falls**

Here's another dandy little day trip from the week-long family camp at Blue Creek Campground (Hike 72). The two little lakes, named Two Little Lakes, sitting amid a circle of forested ridges, climax the walk. They also can be included on an 8½-mile loop via Mad Lake, stretched to 11½ miles by adding a sidetrip to Klone Peak (Hike 76).

From Blue Creek Campground, elevation 5400 feet (Hike 72), take Blue Creek trail No. 1426 through fine, big meadows ½ mile to a junction with trail No. 1417 (Hike 77). Continue straight ahead on Blue Creek trail, at about 1 mile leaving meadows and climbing, sometimes steeply. The first of the Two Little Lakes, Ann, is attained at 5600 feet. The trail gains another 100 feet, then drops to the larger of the two, Louise, 5500 feet.

An ancient trail shelter is attractive only to folks in dire straits, but the camping in the vicinity is tolerable. The lakes are best looked at and photographed, being shallow and muddy-bottomed, worthless for wading and not all that attractive for drinking.

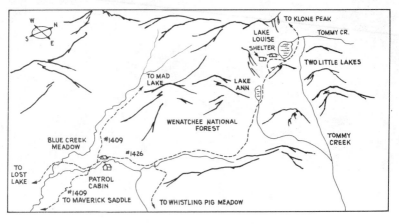

Trail shelter at Louise Lake

Summit of Klone Peak

CHIWAWA RIVER
Unprotected area

76   KLONE PEAK LOOP

**Loop trip from Blue Creek
  Campground 11½ miles (from
  Maverick Saddle 20½ miles)
Hiking time 6 hours
High point 6820 feet
Elevation gain 1500 feet**

**Hikable July through September
One day
USGS Chikamin Creek and Silver
  Falls**

One of the two lookout cabins which once watched over Mad River country stood atop Klone Peak, 6820 feet. The cabin is gone but the panoramas are as grand as ever: forest, mountains, and even, on the far horizon, the Columbia River Plateau. The meadows along the way are, in themselves, sufficient reason to do what is, after all, not so terribly strenuous a walk, though long.

From Blue Creek Campground (Hike 72), elevation 5400 feet, hike Blue Creek trail No. 1426 the 2 miles to Two Little Lakes (Hike 75) and drop a hundred feet to a crossing of Tommy Creek, 5400 feet. The forested way is now all up, some stretches steep, some of the switchbacks ridiculously flat, built that way to try to reduce motorcycle and horse erosion in the soft soil of Glacier Peak pumice. At 6200 feet, 4 miles from the campsite, is a junction with North Tommy Ridge trail No. 1425 (Hike 80). Numbers on an old sign here may not be the same as on the new Forest Service map.

Turn right on trail No. 1425, past small waterfalls, and in 1¼ miles turn left on Klone Peak trail No. 1427 a short distance to the summit of Klone Peak, 5½ miles from Blue Creek Campground. To the north are Glacier Peak, Clark Mountain, Ten Peak. East are Duncan Hill and Pyramid Mountain. South is farm country. Southwest is Mt. Stuart and a tiny bit of Mt. Rainier.

To complete the loop, go 1½ miles back to Blue Creek trail No. 1426 and turn right, mostly through woods, 1 mile to a junction in Marble Meadows with Mad River trail No. 1409. Turn right 1 mile to the Mad Lake trail, a mandatory sidetrip, ¼ mile each way (Hike 72). Proceed in a succession of meadows to Blue Creek Campground, for a total of 11½ miles.

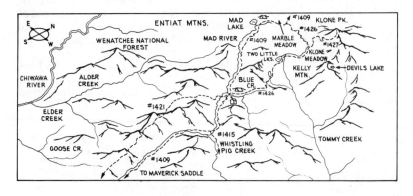

77 WHISTLING PIG LOOP

**Loop trip from Blue Creek
  Campground 6 miles
Hiking time 4 hours
High point 6100 feet
Elevation gain 900 feet**

**Hikable July to mid-October
One day
USGS Silver Falls**

A huge meadow and views across the Entiat River valley are the botanical and scenic rewards. The spice of history is provided by an ancient log cabin. As for wildlife, listen for the whistling of the pigs, as the old mountain men called marmots. This trip makes an excellent day trip from Blue Creek Campground, but it can also be a 15-mile loop from Maverick Saddle.

From Blue Creek Campground (Hike 72), elevation 5400 feet, hike Mad River trail No. 1409 downstream toward Maverick Saddle. In 1¼ miles, at 5200 feet, lowest point on the loop, turn left on Tyee Ridge trail No. 1415.

The trail climbs steadily ¾ mile and splits. Straight ahead is the way to Cougar Mountain (Hike 74). Go left on Hunters trail No. 1417 the ½ mile (2½ miles from Blue Creek Campground) to the edge of Whistling Pig Meadow, 5700 feet. Cross to a large grove of trees, site of the old log cabin and the campsites.

The trail enters forest and intersects Middle Tommy Creek trail No. 1424 at 5900 feet. Turn left, contouring a steep hillside to a high point at 6100 feet. Near here spot a naked knoll to the right; leave the trail and climb a short bit to the edge of a cliff and views to mountains across the Entiat valley.

The slope of the hillside gentles out and the trail descends into Blue Creek drainage, passing East Blue Creek Meadow. At 5½ miles from the start turn left on Blue Creek trail No. 1426 and return to Blue Creek Campground at 6 miles.

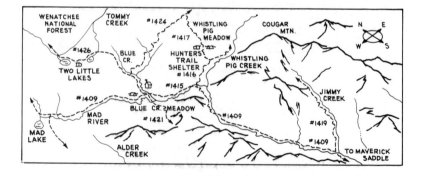

(Opposite) Whistling Pig Meadow

CHIWAWA RIVER
Unprotected area

78 ENTIAT MOUNTAINS VIEW

Round trip from Maverick Saddle
  25 miles
Allow 2 days
High point 6500 feet
Elevation gain 2300 feet

Hikable July to early October
USGS Chikamin Creek and
  Lucerne

No single spectacle makes this trip notable. All it has to offer is miles and miles of meadows rich in flowers and a series of pretty little creeks—and at the end, a view in one direction over the Chiwawa valley to Glacier Peak, in the other down to the deeps of the Entiat valley. The length of the trail rules out short-legged hikers. The fact that only the last ½ mile is ORV-free means you must keep a tight rein on your temper.

Close inspection shows that motorcycles use these green lawns to make speed runs and little circles. The majority of ORV-riders are responsible people; only a fraction are hooligans. However, not many fools and vandals are required to devastate fragile subalpine terrain; the wounds in the soft soil of Glacier Peak's fields of pumice will remain long after the ecocriminals have gone to their reward. But let not hikers be holier than thou; feet are nowhere near so ruinous as wheels, but they can contribute to the problem. Except for very good reason, always stay on trails.

Drive to Maverick Saddle (Hike 72), elevation 4250 feet.

Hike Mad River trail No. 1409 the 6 miles to Blue Creek Campground and a junction. Go straight ahead on the Mad River trail, pass the sidetrail to Mad Lake at 8 miles (Hike 72), and at 9 miles intersect trail No. 1426 (Hike 77). Continue straight ahead on the Mad River trail, past Marble Meadow, to a junction with trail No. 1409.2, coming from Chikamin Ridge. Keep straight ahead, past Pond Meadow, into the headwaters of Three Creek. To this point there are a number of wayside camps with plenty of water.

Stay on the Mad River trail, which loses 200 feet, contours, and climbs again. At about 10½ miles cross a small stream on a steep slope. Several switchbacks farther along pass a small meadow, then a larger one, the same stream flowing through them. This is the only camp with year-round water for the next 9 miles.

The trail climbs to 6200 feet, drops 100 feet, and again climbs. At 12 miles, 6300 feet, are a junction with the Shetipo trail, the official end of the Mad River trail, and the legal stopping point for motorcycles (heh! heh!). Your way continues straight ahead on what now is Garland Peak trail No. 1408 (Hike 84), becoming very steep, then leveling off to a first look at Glacier Peak, screened by trees. Leave the trail and walk up the 6500-foot knoll for the promised views.

You needn't stop here, of course. The viewpoint is merely the first such along the crest of the Entiat Mountains into the Glacier Peak Wilderness. The next year-round water is 7 miles farther on, at Cow Creek Pass. Beyond it are Larch Lakes at 9 miles, Pomas Pass at 15, and the trail-end at the junction with Ice Creek trail, 17 miles from the 6500-foot viewpoint.

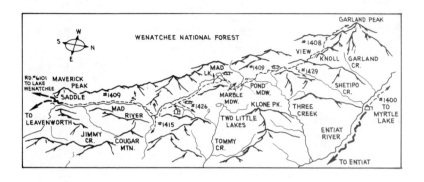

Marble Meadow

Silver forest from the 1970 Entiat Fire on Tyee Ridge

ENTIAT RIVER
Unprotected area

79 TYEE RIDGE—BOILING SPRINGS

Round trip 11 miles
Allow 2 days
High point 6750 feet
Elevation gain 800 feet in, 1700
  feet out

Hikable mid-June to October
USGS Silver Falls, Brief, Tyee
  Mountain

Grueling, that's one word for this high-in-the-sky ridge ramble. Exciting, that's another. The first 4 miles weave in and out of an area hit by the 1970 Entiat Fire, one of the biggest of recent years. The blackened snags on the crest are transforming to a silver forest that will, in years to come, keep your camera clicking or buzzing or whatever it does. Then there are the views—down 4000 feet into Entiat valley, over miles of forested ridges, south to the Stuart Range, north to Glacier Peak. That's the "exciting." The "grueling" is that though all ridge trails have ups and downs, this one goes crazy, losing and gaining 300 to 400 feet at a crack, often with extreme steepness.

From Entiat on the Columbia River drive 9.5 miles on the Entiat River road to Ardenvoir. After .2 mile more, turn left on Mad River road, which eventually becomes road No. 5700. At Pine Flats Campground, 6 miles, the Mad River road leaves the river and climbs another 10 miles. At about 16 miles from the Entiat River road go right on road No. 5713 for 4.7 miles (the last 3 miles may be too rough for a family car) to the last switchback below Tyee Lookout and the start of Tyee Ridge trail No. 1415, elevation 6500 feet.

The trail begins on a firebreak slashed and gouged in 1970. A descent of ¾ mile intersects the abandoned Mott trail, which at 1 mile hits a 6100-foot low point. At 1¾ miles pass Billy Creek trail No. 1416 and climb to a 6500-foot high point. Descend steeply, then ascend moderately steeply to a 6750-foot shoulder of Signal Peak, 6998 feet, and the first good look at Glacier Peak.

Descend (with one little up-blip of 150 feet) past an abandoned trail and at an estimated 5½ miles (the sign guesses 6¼) reach Boiling Springs Meadow, elevation 5900 feet, a sheer joy. The camps are pleasant. The water bubbling from the ground is fun to watch and from the number of tracks, a great place to see deer.

The trail continues on, climbing another 400 feet, passes South Tommy Creek trail No. 1423, and joins the Cougar Mountain trail. At 3¼ miles from Boiling Springs, having lost 1100 feet, intersect the Mad River trail at 1½ miles from Blue Creek Campground (Hike 72).

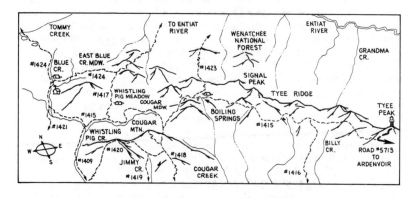

80 NORTH TOMMY RIDGE

Round trip 13 miles
Hiking time 7 hours
High point 6820 feet
Elevation gain 3100 feet in, 700 feet out

Hikable July through October
One day
USGS Silver Falls

Each of five high points on North Tommy Ridge has grand panoramas of mountains and farms and makes a satisfying turnaround. Of course, the farthest and highest (the old fire-lookout site atop Klone Peak) is the bestest.

Until 1986 the second mile of this trail was extremely rough, steep, and difficult. Consequently, the route was seldom used by motorcycles and ORVs; the few that did dug deep into the soft pumice soil, instituting drainage channels that snowmelt trenched knee-deep, utterly destroying long stretches of tread. Rather than recognize that pumice country is no place for high-speed wheels, the Forest Service obtained $87,776 of Washington State gas-tax money to reconstruct the trail to motorcycle standards. The soft, light soil required the motorcycle trail (expressway) to be built at the 10 percent grade abhorred by hikers; endless switchbacks that even go downhill before turning up will invite shortcuts which become erosion channels. The switchbacks are banked and hardened with concrete blocks so the wheels won't have to slow down. A trail once almost machinefree has become a motorcycle obstacle course (with you, the hiker, as the obstacle). The cheapest and simplest answer to the damage of the past would have been to spend a few hundred dollars to fill the worst of the ruts, put in short stretches of new tread, and prohibit the machines that were ripping up the country. However the motorcyclists persuaded the Forest Service, which never so much as gave hikers a chance to say "NO." Given this egregious example of Forest Service deafness, hikers must start yelling, with letters, written not to the rangers, but to *congressmen* and *senators*.

From Entiat drive 19.7 miles on the Entiat River road and turn left on road No. 5605, signed "North Tommy Trail." In 7.2 miles reach the road-end and the North Tommy trail No. 1425, elevation 4500 feet.

The first mile gains a meager 100 feet to a creek crossing, the only water on the route. Then begins the 10 percent monotony. At 3 miles is the top of the first knoll, 5863 feet, with views from a helipad clearing.

The trail drops 300 feet, climbs 600 feet to the second knoll, loses a bit and gains 100 feet to the third, loses 100 feet and gains 200 to the fourth. You can't quit now.

The path drops 200 feet to a junction with the abandoned Klone Peak trail from the Entiat valley (Hike 81), loses 100 feet along a narrow ridge crest, and bumps against the base of Klone Peak. Climb a final 600 feet, to within a few hundred feet of the summit, and join the Blue Creek trail, a popular route from the Mad River trail. At 6½ miles from the road step out on the lastest and bestest panorama point. The USGS map says the summit is 6820 feet; the sign on top says 6834. The cabin was destroyed by vandals in 1959, but the foundation is still there. So are the views.

View from the first high point on North Tommy Ridge

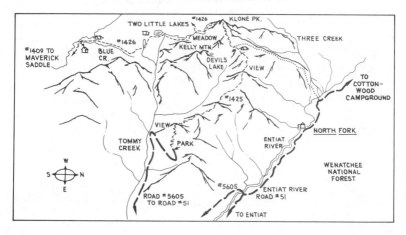

OLD KLONE PEAK TRAIL

Round trip 10 miles
Hiking time 7 hours
High point 6820 feet
Elevation gain 4000 feet

Hikable July through September
One day
USGS Silver Falls

Would you like to reach all that good stuff on Tommy Ridge (Hike 80) with no hassle by machines? This abandoned trail is for you. While struggling over the blowdowns, bless the Forest Service for letting one trail stay motorfree in an area overrun by gas-guzzlers, smoke-poopers, and ditch-gougers. The benefaction didn't cost a nickel of public funds. Nature installed the wheelstops, at no charge. So much for the good news. The bad news is the necessity to cross the Entiat River sans bridge and then to gain 4000 feet of altitude.

From Entiat drive 33 miles (.5 mile beyond the Duncan Ridge road) on the Entiat River road and find the abandoned road leading steeply down to the river and the concrete piers of the old footbridge shown on the USGS map. Some years a logjam or fallen tree spans the flood. If not, give up the trip. The Entiat River is too deep and swift to ford.

Across the river, poke around the concrete pier to find tread of old Klone Peak trail No. 1427 on the bank of Three Creek, elevation 2800 feet.

The trail sticks close to the creek for a scant ½ mile, then switchbacks away; tread thins to nothing at the critical point; scout around for cut-banks and cut logs.

The story from here is switchbacks, 3500 feet gained in 3½ miles, on a broad hillside that narrows to become Three Creek Ridge. Holes open in the forest, giving a good look at Pyramid Mountain and, at the ridge top, a glimpse of Glacier Peak. A short drop leads to a junction with North Tommy trail No. 1425 (Hike 80), 6300 feet, 4 miles from the river. Join the motorcycles for the final short ascent to the top of Klone Peak, 6820 feet (or 6834).

Near the North Tommy junction are campsites, but no water after the snow melts. Carry a gallon from Three Creek.

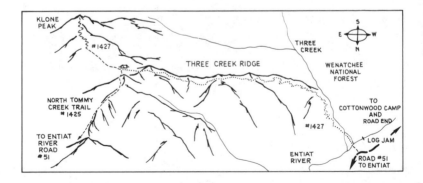

Crossing Entiat River on logjam

Deer on Entiat River trail

ENTIAT RIVER
Unprotected area

DUNCAN HILL

Round trip from road No. 2920
  14 miles
Hiking time 7 hours
High point 7819 feet
Elevation gain 3300 feet
Hikable mid-July through mid-
  October
One day or backpack
USGS Lucerne

Round trip via Anthem Creek
  trail 16½ miles
Hiking time 12 hours
Elevation gain 4700 feet

Sweat and pant and grumble to a former lookout site atop 7819-foot Duncan Hill, and there be richly rewarded for the suffering with views up and down the Entiat Valley, from golden sagebrush hills to the rock-and-snow giants of Mt. Maude and Seven-Fingered Jack. The trail traverses the peak, making possible two quite different routes that can be combined in a superb loop, if transportation can be arranged from one trailhead to another. It is also the opening leg of another fine loop to Milham Pass. To ameliorate the suffering, carry water to compensate for Nature's stinginess.

According to the Forest Service ranger, this trail is so little used by machines or feet you can have a purer wilderness experience here than on the bike-infested Entiat River trail. However, the soft pumice under the Duncan Hill trail has been so sorely grooved by a few motorbike wheels that one must often walk to the side of the trail.

From Entiat on the Columbia River drive the Entiat River road 33 miles (5 miles short of the end at Cottonwood Campground) and near North Fork Campground turn right on road No. 5608. At 5.8 miles (dodging lesser sideroads) stay right at a well-traveled intersection and at 5.9 miles go left a short distance to the trailhead, elevation 4800 feet.

The way sets out along wooded Duncan Ridge, climbing a 5549-foot knob, dropping 100 feet, then climbing again to 5800 feet. The grade moderates and in about 3½ miles enters semi-meadows, with water and good camps, at the head of Duncan Creek. At about 5 miles is a junction; keep right. At 6½ miles is another junction; again keep right and climb to the top of Duncan Hill, 7 miles from the road.

For the second approach, drive all the 38 miles to Cottonwood Campground, elevation 3144 feet. Try this route in May or June. There likely will be too much snow to reach the summit, but the spring flowers and the abundance of does with fawns are worth it. (Look at and photograph them all you want, but never touch.)

Walk Entiat River trail No. 1400 a flattish 2½ miles and turn right, uphill, on Anthem Creek trail No. 1435. Now the fun begins—if your idea of entertainment is endless switchbacks gaining 2400 feet. At 5900 feet, 6 miles from the road, is the junction with Duncan Ridge trail No. 1434. For camping, turn left ¼ mile to water or 1 mile farther to a spot about 500 feet above the crossing of Anthem Creek. For the summit, turn right and climb open scree and flowers; the tread becomes obscure, so watch it. At 7¾ miles is a junction; take the upper trail to the summit, 8¼ miles.

If a party has two cars, or some other ingenious scheme, the two summit approaches make a dandy combination.

For a loop famous for flowers and views, at the 5900-foot junction turn left on Duncan Ridge trail the 6 up-and-down miles to Snowbrushy Creek trail and Milham Pass (Hike 97). Descend to the Entiat River trail and then to the road.

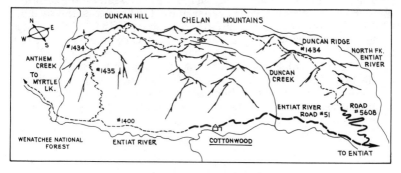

83 MYRTLE LAKE

Round trip 8½ miles
Hiking time 4 hours
High point 3700 feet
Elevation gain 560 feet

Hikable mid-June through
**   October**
One day or backpack
USGS Lucerne

Deep forest of the lower Entiat valley provides an ambling entry to the jade-green lake hidden in a fold of ridges falling from Rampart Mountain. The trail grade is easy, the camping is pleasant, the swimming is bracing. Of all the hikes in the Entiat, this should be an ideal trail for a family with small children. Children? Make sure they look both ways before stepping out on the trail. The Forest Service has made it into a motorcycle track.

During the extremely dry summer of 1985 the fire-spitting machines were banned from the forest, offering hikers a rare opportunity to reacquaint themselves with the area. Wait and watch for such chances. The Entiat is so beautiful it's worth choosing the right time to visit. Of course, enough letters (to *congressmen* and *senators*) can get the machines out of there forever.

From Entiat drive the Entiat River road to its end, .2 mile beyond Cottonwood Camp, elevation 3144 feet.

Hike Entiat River trail No. 1400, through deep forest, distant from the river. Note that as a pedestrian you are a third-class citizen. The trail has been widened for motorcycles and a swath cut through the shade trees to accommodate horses' hips; the walker must sweat in the hot sun, ever alert to jump out of the way of machines doing up to 25 miles per hour—very often in gangs.

When the wheel-and-hoof expressway gets too hot and noisy and stinky, refresh yourself on one of the many sidetrails down to river views and cold water. In 2½ miles, with minor ups and downs netting a mere 400 feet, pass Anthem Creek trail No. 1435, and in ¼ mile more, a sylvan camp at Anthem Creek. Note the wide bridge; before the trail was reconstructed for motorcycles a footlog did the job. The Forest Service has to abandon foot trails for lack of funds, but there's no shortage of money to speed the wheels.

The way pokes along the valley floor, the forest opening here and there for glimpses of Devils Smokestack and Rampart Mountain. At 3½ miles turn left on Cow Creek-Myrtle Lake trail No. 1404 and cross the river on a bridge. In a couple hundred yards the trail splits. Both forks climb, at a slightly steeper pitch, to Myrtle Lake, 3700 feet. For camping take the left fork, which rounds the shore to peaceful forest sites at the south end (wheels are banned). For day hiking take the right fork to the north end of the lake. Gaze upon the serene waters in the lovely forest bowl, greenery interrupted only by cliffs and talus on the west side. Put in your ear plugs (don't do so sooner, lest you fail to hear the hurtling machines). Take a tranquilizer. Compose your letter.

Myrtle Lake

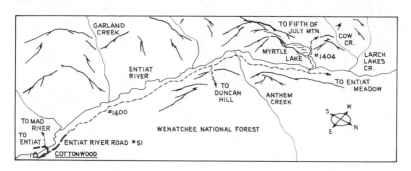

84 SHETIPO CREEK—DEVILS SMOKESTACK LOOP

Loop trip 22¾ miles	Hikable mid-July through
Allow 2–3 days	September
High point 7400 feet	USGS Lucerne and Plain
Elevation gain 6254 feet	

Aside from the intimations of diabolism (the Hell-hued rocks of the volcanic neck thrusting ruggedly through sheer cliffs), this high-country loop has much to daunt the faint heart. The trail is extremely steep in spots and in others next to non-existent. All day you face the barren waste without the taste of water, cool, clear water (water!). After the snow melts, few places on the route have water all summer.

Drive to the end of the Entiat River road (Hike 83), elevation 3144 feet.

Hike to Myrtle Lake, 3700 feet, 4¼ miles (Hike 83). Now the climb begins, switchbacking through deep woods, over a rocky shoulder of Rampart Mountain; a bare knob off the trail to the right gives views to the Entiat valley. The way rounds the corner of the shoulder and eases off, contouring steep walls of Cow Creek valley. At 2 miles beyond Myrtle Lake, 6¼ miles from the road, a spur trail goes left over a little rise to Cow Creek Meadows, 5100 feet, a large parkland flat enclosed by cliffs of Rampart and Fifth of July Mountains. Campsites are numerous. A virtually permanent heap of avalanche snow yields meaningful water.

Again the uphill labor, ameliorated by splendid cross-Entiat views to Duncan Hill, Peak 7936, and Gopher Mountain. At 6000 feet the trail passes a terrific viewpoint on a rock buttress, a campsite, and a path to water. Larch forest commences. At 8½ miles from the road, Cow Creek trail ends by intersecting Garland Peak trail No. 1408, 6500 feet. To the right is a little waterfall creek with several fine camps a short climb above the trail; farther to the right, and down, are the campsites at Larch Lakes (Hike 85), 1½ miles from the intersection.

The loop, however, turns left, abruptly descending a pumice slope, skirting below a band of cliffs, and climbing to Cow Creek Pass (or Fifth of July Pass) 7000 feet, on the shoulder of Fifth of July Mountain. The short scramble to the summit and its commanding views is just about mandatory.

From the shoulder, drop to a 6800-foot saddle; the trail becomes vague to imaginary, the blazes one-half-a-century old. Turn west, traverse to a long rib, and descend to a basin with a small meadow camp—the Ravens Roost—at 5900 feet. There is water all summer, usually. A long uphill swing around the side of Rampart Mountain, then switchbacks, lead to an old sheepherders' camp. Water sometimes. The trail vanishes, reap-

Shetipo Creek trail

Glacier Peak from Garland Peak trail

pears above a clump of trees, and proceeds around Rampart to a narrow saddle, 7100 feet.

The way levels off for a wide-open contour around Devils Smokestack to an exposed knob, 7400 feet, with views to everywhere. This is the highest elevation of the loop. Gaze to your full, then drop the short bit to intersect the Basalt Ridge trail (Hike 60), 13 miles from the start.

The trail sidehills open ground toward Garland Peak, the soil fragile, criss-crossed with confusing animal traces; the correct path climbs briefly, then drops gently as it rounds Garland Peak (Hike 60), another sidetrip essential for view hogs. The way drops, climbs, and drops to a wooded saddle, 6100 feet; a sidetrail leads to Pinto Camp, an agreeable meadow with a very questionable spring.

At 17½ miles the Garland trail ends in a little pass at a junction with Shetipo Creek trail No. 1429, 6300 feet. Motorcycles are permitted to run here; at some corners the tread is rutted so deeply that multiple use is a difficult feat. Zigging and zagging down 5 long miles, the trail enters Cottonwood Campground on the Entiat River. Cross on the car bridge and find a path heading upriver the final ¼ mile to the parking lot, closing the loop at 22¾ miles.

Devils Smokestack from Garland Peak trail

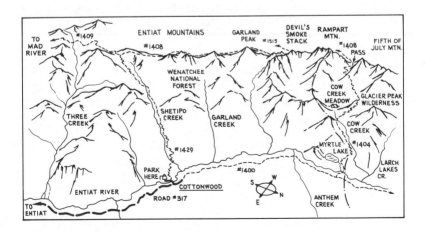

85   LARCH LAKES LOOPS

Round trip (shorter loop) 18 miles
Allow 2–3 days
High point 6500 feet
Elevation gain 3400 feet

Hikable mid-July through
  September
USGS Lucerne

Two clear lakes surrounded by alpine trees and meadows nestled under cliffs of Fifth of July Mountain. An entryway to miles and miles of up-and-down high trails along the Entiat Mountains.

Drive to the end of the Entiat River road (Hike 83), elevation 3144 feet.

Hike Entiat River trail No. 1400 for 5 miles to Larch Lakes trail, 3800 feet. The way crosses the Entiat River, goes ¼ mile through stately forest, and then begins a grueling climb of 1900 feet in 2½ miles, switchbacking up a treeless, shadeless, waterless south slope. On a hot day the best plan is to loiter by the river until late afternoon, when sun has left the hillside—or better yet, cook dinner by the river and make the ascent in the cool of the evening. Waiting until morning does no good; the hillside gets the first rays of sun.

Before starting up, note the waterfall high on the hillside to the west. Elevation of this falls (which comes from the lake outlet) provides a measure of how much climbing remains to be done.

The tortuous switchbacks abruptly flatten into a traverse along the shores of 5700-foot Lower Larch Lake, leading to a large meadow and acres of flat ground for camping. The trail continues a short ½ mile to Upper Larch Lake, more meadows, and the junction with the Pomas Creek trail. Here is a choice of loop trips.

For the longer of the two, climb north some 700 feet to Larch Lakes Pass, then amble on to 6350-foot Pomas Pass and down Pomas Creek to a junction with the Ice Creek trail, 6 miles from Upper Larch Lake. Go left to Ice Lakes (Hike 86) or right to the Entiat River trail.

For the shorter and more popular loop, follow the trail south around Upper Larch Lake. Tread disappears in meadows and several starts can

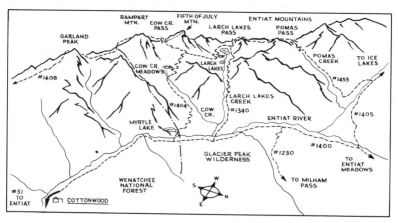

be seen on the wooded hillside left of Fifth of July Mountain. The correct path goes into the woods at the base of the slope a couple of hundred feet from a granite "island" in the meadow.

The trail climbs steadily more than a mile, with airy views down to Larch Lakes, then contours the mountain to a 6500-foot junction with the Cow Creek trail, the return route via Myrtle Lake.

The ascent of Fifth of July Mountain is a must. Though the north face of the peak is a tall, rugged cliff, there's an easy side. Leave packs at the junction and climb the Garland Peak trail a mile south to 7000-foot Cow Creek Pass (some signs say Fifth of July Pass) and ascend the gentle south slope to the 7696-foot summit and a 360-degree panorama of Glacier, Clark, Maude, Rainier, and other peaks beyond counting.

The Cow Creek trail descends a steep 2 miles to the edge of Cow Creek Meadows and another 2 miles via Myrtle Lake (Hike 83) to the Entiat River trail, reached at a point 3½ miles from the road-end.

Upper Larch Lake

86   ENTIAT MEADOWS AND ICE LAKES

Round trip to Lower Ice Lake 28 miles
Allow 3–5 days
High point (knoll above lower lake) 6900 feet
Elevation gain 4200 feet
Hikable August through September
USGS Holden and Lucerne

Round trip to Entiat Meadows 30 miles
Allow 3–4 days or more
High point 5500 feet
Elevation gain 2400 feet
Hikable July through October

A long trail with many byways to glory and at the two ends a pair of climaxes: a vast meadow under small glaciers hanging on the walls of a row of 9000-foot peaks, and two high, remote lakes set in cirque basins close under cliffs of 9082-foot Mt. Maude, with alpine trees standing out starkly in a barren, glaciated landscape reminiscent of Khyber Pass. Mountain goats, too, often stand out in the open.

Drive to the end of the Entiat River road (Hike 83), elevation 3144 feet.

Hike Entiat River trail No. 1400, engineered by the Forest Service the first 4½ miles into a motorcycle expressway; stay alert to avoid being knocked down or run over, especially by unsupervised children. At 3½ miles is the turnoff to the Cow Creek trail and Myrtle Lake, destination of most speed freaks. At 5 miles is the Larch Lakes trail (Hike 85) and at 5½ miles a campsite by Snowbrushy Creek. At 6½ miles, 3900 feet, is a beautiful camp below the trail in a Snowbrushy meadow; here too is the Snowbrushy Creek trail to Milham Pass (Hike 97). At 8¼ miles, 4300 feet, reach the split.

Ice Lakes: The Ice Creek trail goes left a short bit to a camp and a two-log bridge over the river; if the bridge is missing, look upstream for a log. The way climbs gradually in forest the first mile, then drops 400 feet to Ice Creek. At 1½ miles, 4300 feet, is a junction with the Pomas Creek trail, an excellent alternate return route via Larch Lakes (Hike 85).

The route goes along the river bottom, alternating between small alpine trees and meadows. At about 3 miles is a crossing of Ice Creek; since a footlog seldom is available and the channel is too wide to jump, be prepared to wade—and find out how well the creek lives up to its name. In another mile is another crossing, but this time the creek can be stepped over on rocks. At some 4½ miles from the Entiat trail, formal tread ends in a rocky meadow and delightful campsite, 5500 feet. The noisy creek drowns the sound of a pretty waterfall tumbling from Upper Ice Lake.

From the trail-end a boot-built path follows the rocky meadow north to the valley head, passing the waterfall. Generally keep right of the creek, but cross to the left when the going looks easier there. The valley ends in a steep, green hillside; above, in hanging cirques, lie the lakes. From a starting point to the right of the creek, scramble up game traces, crossing the creek and climbing between cliffs to its left. The way emerges onto a

Falls on Ice Creek

rocky knoll 100 feet above 6800-foot Lower Ice Lake, 6 miles from the Entiat trail. Camp on pumice barrens, not the fragile heather; no fires permitted.

Upper Ice Lake is a mile farther. Head southwest in a shallow alpine valley, below cliffs, to the outlet stream and follow the waters up to the 7200-foot lake, beautifully cold and desolate.

Mt. Maude cliffs are impressive from the lakes. However, the long and gentle south ridge of the peak offers an easy stroll. The scramble to the ridge, though, is not a complete cinch; patches of steep snow remain in summer and require an ice ax for safe passage. Maude is the only 9000-footer in the Cascades accessible to hikers, but they must be experienced hikers thoroughly familiar with the ice ax and the rules of safe travel on steep terrain. The summit views extend from Glacier Peak to the Columbia Plateau and from Mt. Rainier to an infinite alpine wilderness north.

Entiat Meadows: The way to the split is principally through forest; the final 7 miles up the Entiat River alternate between trees and meadows. Though sheep have not been allowed in the valley for years, some meadows still show deep rutting from thousands of hooves, and some of the native flowers have never grown back.

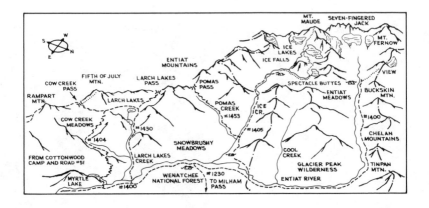

At 13 miles, having gained only some 2000 feet thus far, the grade steepens a little for a final 1¼ miles and then, at about 5500 feet, the tread fades out in fields of heather and flowers. The camps are fine throughout the miles-long Entiat Meadows and the views are grand—up the cliffs of the huge cirque to the summits of Fernow, Seven-Fingered Jack, and Maude, all above 9000 feet, and to remnants of the Entiat Glacier, which in days of glory excavated the cirque and gave the valley its contours.

If ambition persists, scramble up grassy slopes of the ridge to the north and look down into Railroad Creek and the town of Holden.

Lunch stop in Entiat Meadows

Entiat Meadows and Mount Maude

87   LAKE CREEK BASIN

Round trip 6 miles   **Hikable June to mid-October**
Hiking time 3 hours   **One day or backpack**
High point 4800 feet   **USGS Brief**
Elevation gain 900 feet

No lakes. No views. Nothing to brag about except miles of wandering through forest of lodgepole pine to a grove of giant fir trees and a pleasant camp beside a nice little stream. Beware of hot wheels; this is still another trail the Forest Service has converted, using your gas-tax dollars, into an obstacle course of the sort beloved of the wheelers. (You, the hiker, are the obstacle.)

From Entiat drive about 19 miles on the Entiat River road and turn right on road No. 5900, signed "Lake Chelan." In 2.7 miles is a major switchback; a spur road with a trail sign takes off here. Either park above the switchback at an elevation of 4000 feet or, if the spur is passable, drive straight ahead .2 mile, to a large parking area, elevation 3900 feet.

Lake Creek trail No. 1443 begins on an abandoned logging road (which may be reopened). In about 1 mile true trail commences. At 2 miles cross Lake Creek on a footlog and at about 3 miles come to a junction with trail No. 1445, 4800 feet. Here are the campsite and stream, the recommended turnaround.

If further easy strolling in the lodgepoles suits your mood, continue on Lake Creek trail, climbing and then descending to another crossing of Lake Creek at 4 miles. Alternately, follow trail No. 1445 to the top of Angle Peak, 6700 feet, on the Devils Backbone trail.

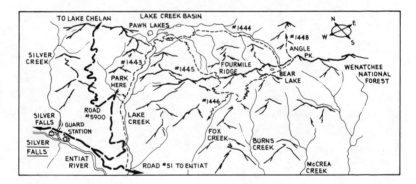

Lodgepole pine forest and Lake Creek trail

88 DEVILS BACKBONE

Round trip 9 miles
Hiking time 5 hours
High point 7100 feet
Elevation gain 1000 feet in, 600
feet out

Hikable July to October
One day
USGS Stormy Mountain

Between the deep valley of the Entiat River and the deep glacial trough of Lake Chelan lies a ridge that splits the sky. The views from a 7100-foot high point run clear over the horizons toward the end of the world. But before jumping in your boots and strapping on your rucksack, read on.

The run along the ridge once matched the grand background with a lovely subalpine foreground. It will again, in a century or so. Since the Entiat Fire of 1970, however, the "trail" has consisted of truck ruts and cat-gouged firebreak. Moreover, the "trail" has been "improved" to motorcycle standards; ergo, dust inches deep.

The Devils Backbone wheelway is the focal point of 75 miles of Forest Service motorcycle mainlines in the Chelan Mountains south of Shady Pass. Regrading these one-time foot trails was subsidized by the Washington State gas tax to the extent of $6000 a mile. (A motorcycle travels 40 to 60 miles a day using about 2 gallons of gas, so how many motorcycles generating 36 cents in gas-tax money per day does it take to pay for 40 to 60 miles of trail?) The economics don't concern the Forest Service trail bosses in this area; they are using your gas-tax money, not theirs. Neither does the cost bother the officials of the state of Washington who hold the public purse strings; they have more gas-tax money dedicated to ORVs than places to spend it. The following trails are part of the Devils Backbone ORV system: Lake Creek trail (Hike 87), 6.8 miles; Angle Peak, 4 miles; Fourmile Ridge, 6 miles; Chelan Summit, 11.5 miles; North Fork Twentyfive Mile Creek, 8 miles; Pot Peak, 10 miles; Trail No. 1449, 2 miles; Lone Peak, 10 miles; Stormy Creek, 8.2 miles; Fox Creek, 3.7 miles; and Burns Creek, 4.3 miles. Until these last two are rebuilt, they are hiker-only.

From Entiat drive about 19 miles on the Entiat River road and turn right on road No. 5900, signed "Lake Chelan," for 14 miles. (The same point can be reached by driving 15 miles from Lake Chelan on Twentyfive Mile Creek road.) Turn onto road No. (5900)114 for .3 mile and turn right on No. (5900)118 to the end of drivable road, elevation 6600 feet.

Devils Backbone trail No. 1448 climbs ruts steeply, then levels off in an easy stretch to a 6900-foot high point. A discouraging 200 feet are lost, and three more times the ups are succeeded by downs. At 3½ miles is a junction; go right on Fourmile trail No. 1445 another 1 mile to within a stone's throw of the 7100-foot high point on Fourmile Ridge. Do it in the quiet of midweek and you may not have to share the inspiring views with noisy motors.

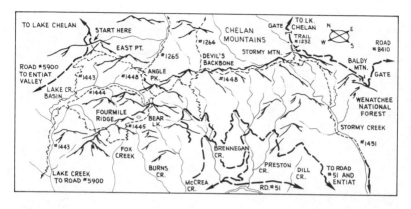

Fourmile trail

Pyramid Mountain trail on the side of Crow Hill

89 BIG HILL—PYRAMID MOUNTAIN

Round trip 18 miles
Hiking time 10 hours
High point 8245 feet
Elevation gain 3100 feet in, 1400
feet out

Hikable mid-July to mid-
September
One day or backpack
USGS Lucerne and Silver Falls

Spectacular, yes, walking a ridge so high it almost touches the sky, looking out through miles of empty air to Glacier Peak, lording it over an infinity of icy-craggy attendants. The supreme moment is standing where once the lookout cabin did, atop Pyramid Mountain, with an airplane-wing view 7000 feet straight down to blue waters of Lake Chelan. However, a word to the thrifty: If the summit of Pyramid is your main goal, you do better to get there via South Pyramid Creek (Hike 93), saving much wear and tear on the family car; the road to Big Hill trailhead varies from bad to atrocious.

From the Entiat River road drive road No. 5900 (Hike 88), which is often dusty and rutted, always steep and narrow. At 8.4 miles keep left at Shady Pass on road No. (5900)112. At 10.2 miles pass Big Hill. Keep left on road No. (5900)113 to the road-end and trailhead, 10.7 miles from the Entiat, elevation 6550 feet.

Pyramid Mountain trail No. 1433 sets out on a wide firebreak slashed to keep busy while waiting for the rains to come and put out the 1970 Entiat Fire. It climbs around the first bump, passes Poodle Dog Camp, and at about 1½ miles climbs to a 7000-foot high point on Crow Hill. A heartbreaking drop ensues, to 6200 feet. At 3 miles pass Butte Creek trail and a nice camp at the head of Butte Creek. A gutwrenching climb goes to 7000 feet on flower-meadow Graham Mountain. Again (sob!) a drop to 6600 feet. At 6 miles is a junction and another camp with water. Turn right on Pyramid View trail No. 1441 and at 9 miles step proudly onto the summit of Pyramid Peak, 8245 feet, and enjoy your promised reward.

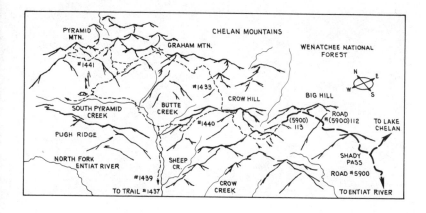

90 NORTH FORK ENTIAT RIVER

Round trip to trail-end 16 miles (to Fern Lake junction 12 miles)
Allow 2 days
High point 6600 feet
Elevation gain 2600 feet

Hikable July through October
USGS Lucerne

The North Fork Entiat River country has 43 miles of trails, offering dramatic views, subalpine meadows, loud streams—and, thanks to Wenatchee National Forest, mobs of motorcycles. That must not be permitted to continue. Letters must be written to your congressman. Angry

Alpine meadow near end of North Fork Entiat River trail

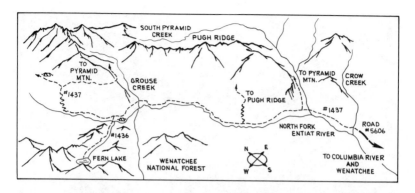

noises made. The chorus must come from beginning hikers who want to enjoy in peace the lovely walks in the low valleys, from intermediates ambitious to take off on a glorious ridge run starting from one of the highest roads in the state, and from experienced highlanders fond of the strenuous climb to an old lookout site. The main thoroughfare is a forest trail passing through several small meadows to a delightful camp beside a little stream with a big name—North Fork Entiat River. Here is a fine base for day hikes.

From Entiat drive the Entiat River road 32.5 miles and turn right 4.1 miles on road No. 5606 to North Fork Entiat trail No. 1437, elevation 4000 feet.

The trail immediately crosses Crow Creek and, after some ups and downs, South Pyramid Creek at 1 mile. At 1¼ miles pass the South Pyramid Creek trail (Hike 93) and at 2¾ miles, the Pugh Ridge trail (Hike 91). At about 4 miles small meadows begin to break the forest; come early for the flowers. At 5 miles the trail becomes very steep and stays that way to Fern Lake junction, 5300 feet, 6 miles; here is that delightful camp by the river, the spot to lay out a mountain home.

After 1 more upstream mile the path again tilts very steeply, gaining 1000 feet in ¾ mile. At 8 miles from the road it ends at a junction with the Pyramid Mountain trail, 6600 feet. Go left a short bit to a large meadow with fine camps, more mountain homes.

Are your legs still jittering for exercise? Take the Pyramid Mountain trail 2 miles to Saska Pass, 7425 feet, and views down Snowbrushy Creek and the North Fork valley.

Alpine meadow on top of Pugh Ridge

NORTH FORK ENTIAT RIVER
Unprotected area

PUGH RIDGE

Round trip 12 miles
Hiking time 9 hours
High point 6783 feet
Elevation gain 2800 feet

Hikable July to mid-October
One day
USGS Lucerne

The close views of the giant peaks around Milham Pass are a joy forever, and they're only part of the scenery. The meadows are very good,
too. The trail is rough, at a steep angle. So much the better, giving a de-

gree of freedom from the fume-spewing, racket-making monsters which infest the region. But only "a degree." On our hike we saw few traces of motorcycles, until three of them came churning up the hill, gouging deep ruts at every switchback. They showed not the least concern for the damage they were doing.

Drive North Fork Entiat River road No. 5606 (Hike 90) to North Fork Entiat trail No. 1437, elevation 4000 feet.

Hike the North Fork trail 2¾ miles to the Pugh Ridge trail, 4300 feet, and turn right, steeling yourself to gain 2500 feet in 3 miles. The opening ¾ mile switchbacks 800 feet; that average rate of gain is maintained. At 1¼ miles is a nice streamside camp. Nearing timberline the tread grows fainter and in the meadowlands is lost altogether. No matter. Continue up in the open until there is no more up. At 6 miles from the road sit down atop Pugh Ridge at 6783 feet. To the north is the magnificent line of Saska, Emerald, and Cardinal Peaks, all about 8500 feet. East are the naked slopes of Pyramid Mountain (Hike 89). West are the crags of Duncan Hill (Hike 82). In the middle distance is the Devils Smokestack.

For the loop, cross the summit meadow and find the trail down a bit on the west side. Don't leave the meadow until certain you really have the trail underfoot. It drops several hundred feet, climbs to a 7000-foot high point, and descends to an intersection, 8 miles from the road, with trail No. 1433, called the Pyramid Mountain trail though it never goes to the mountain.

Turn downhill to another intersection. Keep straight, continuing down on Pyramid Creek trail No. 1439 (Hike 94) to the North Fork Entiat trail at 1¼ miles from the road, for a loop total of 14½ miles.

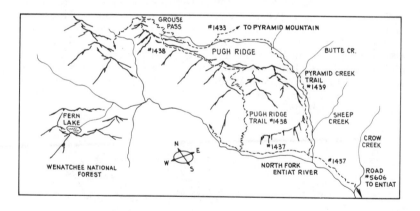

FERN LAKE

Round trip 15 miles
Allow 2 days
High point 6800 feet
Elevation gain 2800 feet

Hikable mid-July through
September
USGS Lucerne

As something of a geological curiosity, Fern Lake is the only lake in North Fork Entiat drainage. Why just this single cirque cupping deep water? Not enough snow in the last few "little ice ages" to crank up the glaciers? The shores might be expected to be a three-deep ring of fishermen. However, the extremely difficult trail (for a mercy, signed "Hiker Only") keeps out the pikers.

Hike North Fork Entiat trail No. 1437 (Hike 90), trailhead elevation 4000 feet, the 6 miles to Fern Creek trail junction, 5300 feet. The camp here is very pleasant and there isn't another spot before the lake to lay your weary bones. The question, therefore, is whether to day-hike from this base or carry packs the 1½ extremely steep miles to the lake, where very few bones can find space.

Cross the North Fork Entiat River—dwindled here to a creek—on an upstream log, and start the switchbacks. Don't complain about the numerous windfalls—as the tire marks everywhere hereabouts testify, the only thing that keeps scofflaw machines off this trail is the succession of down logs, or "wheelstops" as they are known to wildland Luddites.

About halfway up, the trail leaves forest and climbs steeply beside the lake's outlet, tumbling so steeply it's practically all waterfall. The ascent ends abruptly on the shore of the lake, 6800 feet, ringed by ice-scoured cliffs and slabs and buttresses. The little campsite is such a joy you'll be sorry if you took the course of prudence and left your overnight gear below. What's a couple of hours of donkey misery beside a night and morning living in such glory?

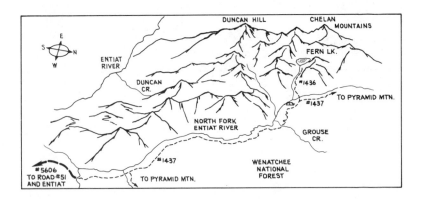

Glacier-smoothed rocks at Fern Lake

93 PYRAMID MOUNTAIN

Round trip 19 miles
Allow 2 days
High point 8247 feet
Elevation gain 4500 feet

Hikable mid-July through
September
USGS Lucerne

The views from this old lookout site extend over range upon range of snow mountains in the Glacier Peak Wilderness, over heat-hazy plateaus of the Columbia Basin, and straight down 7000 feet to Lake Chelan, so far below that binoculars are needed to spot the *Lady of the Lake*. One has to wonder why the place was chosen for a fire lookout—the scenery is all rock, ice, and water, hardly anything in sight that might burn.

The two ways to Pyramid Mountain are the same length and have about the same elevation gain. The route from Big Hill (Hike 89) is spectacular, but the drive to the trailhead is so long and difficult that the recommended route, described here, is the South Pyramid Creek trail, featuring an interesting transition from valley forest to mountain barren.

Thanks to the Forest Service the area is overrun with machines. The hiking trail was rebuilt with wide tread; little creeks were provided with big sturdy bridges; and fords of big creeks were graded to a smoothness permitting wheels to splash through without slowing. Even so, hikers continue to be the majority here; to receive justice, they're going to have to do some yelling about the tyranny of the minority. The yelling will have to be to congressmen—the rangers aren't listening.

Hike North Fork Entiat trail No. 1437 (Hike 90), trailhead elevation 4000 feet. In 1 mile cross Pyramid Creek and at 1¼ miles turn right on South Pyramid Creek trail No. 1439. At 5½ miles, 5800 feet, are the last creekside campsites. At the junction here go right on Pyramid Mountain trail No. 1433, climbing 1¼ miles to another junction; go left here on Pyramid Viewpoint trail No. 1441. An up-and-down traverse emerges

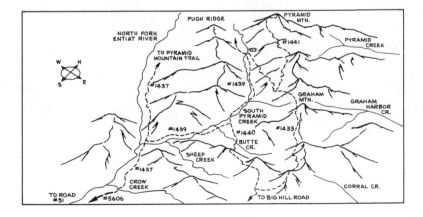

from trees, reaches a small campsite in ½ mile, and yields to steep and steeper tread climbing to the 8246-foot summit, 9½ miles from the road.

Artifacts of the vanished lookout abound: the leveled summit, scraps of metal, and an open-air privy that may have the most spectacular view of any such facility in the Northwest.

Hitching post on top of Pyramid Mountain, overlooking Lake Chelan

94 SOUTH PYRAMID CREEK LOOP

Round trip 18 miles
Allow 2–3 days
High point 7150 feet
Elevation gain 3200 feet

Hikable July through October
USGS Lucerne

Forest, meadows, views, choice camps, a babbling stream. What more? In early summer, flowers and love are in bloom. In late September, larches are old gold, the best kind. The loop can be done either way, of

Grouse beside South Pyramid trail

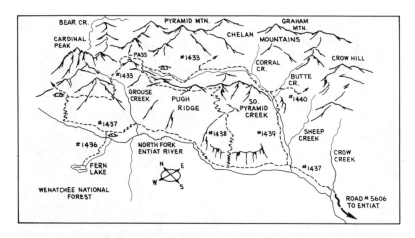

course, but to avoid climbing an extremely steep mile while wearing a heavy pack, it is described here counterclockwise

Set out on North Fork Entiat trail No. 1437 (Hike 90), trailhead elevation 4000 feet. In 1¼ miles turn right on South Pyramid Creek trail No. 1439, whose steep sections happily are short. At about 2½ miles from the road cross the creek on a log. At a bit past 3 miles cross Butte Creek and soon after, South Pyramid Creek—with difficulty, repeated at a recrossing in ½ mile.

At 5¼ miles from the road the South Pyramid Creek trail ends at a junction with Pyramid Mountain trail No. 1433. Keep straight ahead, proceeding up the valley. The way steepens and crosses the stream twice more, but the labors are more than adequately compensated by meadows, views, and choice camps.

At 6¾ miles pass Pugh Ridge trail (see Hike 91 for a shorter loop). At 7 miles cross a saddle in Pugh Ridge, 7150 feet. The trail drops to a crossing of Grouse Creek, 6600 feet, 8½ miles; traverses a steep, broad-view hillside; and at 10 miles intersects North Fork Entiat River trail No. 1437, 6600 feet (Hike 90).

If ready to camp, stay on the Pyramid Mountain trail several hundred yards to a broad meadow flat. Otherwise follow the North Fork trail steeply down (the reason for not doing the loop clockwise) to camps at 11 miles, and more at 12 miles, at the Fern Lake junction (Hike 92). The loop continues downvalley to the junction of South Pyramid Mountain Creek trail at 16¾ miles and the trailhead at 18 miles.

Falls on Butte Creek

NORTH FORK ENTIAT RIVER
Unprotected area

95 BUTTE CREEK—CROW HILL

Round trip 13 miles
Hiking time 2 days
High point 7366 feet
Elevation gain 3400 feet

Hikable early June to mid-
 October
USGS Lucerne

From Crow Hill you only need a springboard to do a swan dive into Lake Chelan, a vertical mile below. If that's not your pleasure, gaze to the circle of large mountains, icy mountains, naked mountains, brown mountains, and green mountains. But if this view is your sole goal, you can achieve it in 1 scant mile from road No. 5900 (Hike 89)—if the road is drivable. The extra attraction here is the *getting* there on a trail so steep it is legally closed to motorcycles. (In this area, where motorcycles physically *can* go, they are legally *allowed* to go.)

Hike North Fork Entiat trail No. 1437 (Hike 90), trailhead elevation 4000 feet, for 1¼ miles and turn right on South Pyramid Creek trail No. 1439 another 2 miles to the junction of Butte Creek trail No. 1440, 4800 feet. Because of the steepness to come, it is recommended that hikers camp at the crossing of South Pyramid Creek (the nicest place) or of Butte Creek, in order to be carrying only a day pack for the morning's ascent, 1800 feet in 2 miles.

Due to its steepness (certainly not from any consideration for hikers) the Butte Creek trail is closed to motorcycles; the Forest Service plans to rebuild the trail for wheels.

Near the top of the first steep pitch, spot a magnificent waterfall, almost hidden in the greenery. In about ½ mile cross Butte Creek, wet your face, and resume wetting your back and brow with sweat. At about 1¼ miles the trail, still steep, comes to a ridge with the beginning of views. At about 1¾ miles it levels and tread all but disappears in a short drop to a junction with Pyramid Mountain trail No. 1433, 6300 feet.

Had enough? If so, meander the short distance to the top of the 6653-foot knoll you have just passed. Great views! Not enough? Turn right on Pyramid Mountain trail, steeply up to a 7000-foot high point. Where the path levels, leave it and stroll open meadows to the top of Crow Hill, 7366 feet. Examine the remains of the ancient cabin. In view of how badly eroded the terrain is by animals, one speculates this was a sheepherder's shelter.

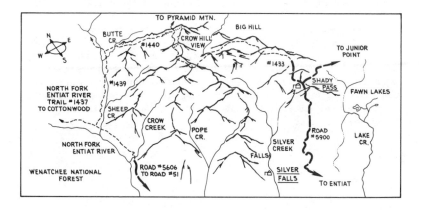

96   DOMKE LAKE

Round trip 6 miles
Hiking time 3 hours
High point 2200 feet
Elevation gain 1100 feet

Hikable June through October
One day or backpack
USGS Lucerne

The trail gives some fine views of Lake Chelan. The lake at trail's end, Domke, has fish (and for each one, three fishermen). Children for whom no summer is complete without a swim but for whom Chelan is too refreshing find Domke sufficiently warm by mid-July for hours of splashing. Though the trip is short enough to be an easy day, families often backpack to spend a lazy week, either camping at trail's end or renting a boat to reach private sites across the lake. As for other entertainment, the odds are that one fisherman in three may get lucky.

Drive to Chelan town or Field Point on Lake Chelan and board the *Lady of the Lake*. For current schedules and fares, call the National Park Service-U.S. Forest Service Information Center in Seattle. The present pattern is daily service from late spring to early fall, dwindling to three boats a week in midwinter; the summer departure time from Chelan town is 8:30 a.m., from Field Point 9:45 a.m., but the schedule could change. In late morning debark at Lucerne, elevation 1096 feet.

Walk the road several hundred feet, cross Railroad Creek, and within ¼ mile find Domke Lake trail No. 1280. The dry and dusty way climbs 250 feet to a great view of Lake Chelan. Forest then closes in, thinning enough at about 1½ miles for more views. At about 2¼ miles is a split. The Emerald Park trail (Hike 97) goes straight ahead; turn left. Ups and downs lead to the private concessionaire's buildings and bathing beach and rental boats at 2¾ miles. The public campground is at 3 miles, 2200 feet.

If views are the goal, at 1 mile from the Lucerne dock go left on Domke Mountain trail No. 1280A, a seldom-used 4½-mile path gaining 3000 feet to the former site of a fire lookout on the summit, 4100 feet. The building, long gone, was perched atop a 110-foot steel tower. To see the same views one must roam from side to side of the rounded mountain— rounded because the ancient Chelan Glacier rode right over the top, meanwhile gouging out the side-channel now occupied by Domke Lake.

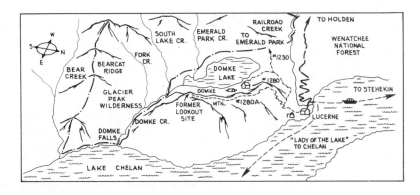

Domke Lake

97 EMERALD PARK

Round trip 16 miles
Allow 2–3 days
High point 5404 feet
Elevation gain 4300 feet

Hikable July to October
USGS Lucerne

The jagged giants clustered about Milham Pass—Saska, Cardinal, and Emerald, all about 8500 feet—catch the eye from afar. At the base of their cliffs is a meadow valley so richly green that when seen from a distance, such as a viewpoint in the Sawtooth Range across Lake Chelan, it seems an impossible dream. Of the many hikers who have had the vision, relatively few achieve the reality because access from one direction, the Entiat valley, is guarded by Milham Pass, 6663 feet, often plugged up with snow until mid-August, and from the other by the expense and inconvenience of travel on Lake Chelan. Though the hiking mileage from the lake makes a reasonable 2-day and easy 3-day trip, boat complications either add a day or two or keep hikers in a constant sweat worrying about connections. Lovely as the meadow is, there's not much exploring to be done unless one has the mountain competence to cope with Milham Pass.

Take the *Lady of the Lake* to Lucerne (Hike 96), elevation 1096 feet.

Hike Domke Lake trail No. 1280. At the lake junction, 2¼ miles, go straight ahead. (However, due to the midday start, you may wish to spend the first night at Domke Lake.) At about 3 miles from the dock pass the Railroad Creek trail. The way contours a steep hillside, in spots angling upward quite strenuously, gives glimpses of Domke Lake, and rounds the corner into the valley of Emerald Park Creek. The trail stays far above the water, whose sound is tantalizing as a dream on those sultry days when the flies go mad with blood lust. Openings in the forest

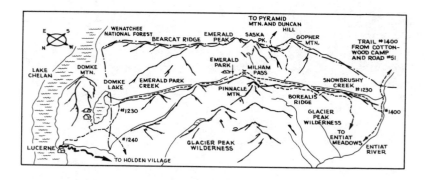

Emerald Park from Milham Pass

begin and grow larger, the sun baking resins from the snowbrush, suffusing the air with the distinctive *"Ceanothus* reek."

At about 6½ miles the trail levels out some and enters a meadow purple with asters, ringed by mountain ash. At 7 miles is a nice streamside camp, 5000 feet. In 1 more mile are larger meadows—the emerald gleam that so entrances the eye when seen from the high ridges across Lake Chelan.

The trail continues to Milham Pass, easy and safe after the snow melts, and with meadows not so jewel-lush, more of the rock-garden variety, but with big views across Lake Chelan to the Sawtooths; the drier climate here supports a distinctly smaller bug population. If a two-car switch can be arranged, or a friend recruited to do the pickup, the best way to do this country is with a one-way hike, exiting via the Entiat River trail (Hike 86).

227

98   LYMAN LAKES

Round trip 20 miles   **Hikable July through September**
Allow 2–3 days   **USGS Holden**
High point 6000 feet
Elevation gain 2700 feet

Ever since Professor Lyman conducted his investigations of the glaciers at the turn of the century, the Lyman Lakes have been perhaps the single most popular spot in the Glacier Peak area. Long before any but a few had heard of Image Lake, packtrains with as many horses as the Sioux had at Little Big Horn were hauling summer-outing hordes up from Lake Chelan via Lucerne or Stehekin, or over the passes from the Entiat River and the Suiattle River. The lakes seem to be on the way to anywhere, or not far off the track. The sidetrip from the Pacific Crest Trail is short. Climbers basecamp to do the big peaks. Off-trail explorers cross the dramatic pass from Spider Meadow.

The quick (not very) access is to take the *Lady of the Lake* to Lucerne (Hike 96) and upon debarking, pay the folks of Holden Village (an old mining town which once was the largest single customer of the Washington State Liquor Commission and now is run by the Lutheran Church as a Christian retreat/resort) to ride their bus to the village, elevation 3300 feet.

It will be well along into afternoon by the time you have hiked the road the 1 mile from the village to Holden Campground; the notion of spending the first night here will have some appeal, though other camps are situated at short intervals up the Railroad Creek valley. A hiker in this valley will gain the impression that a major segment of the population of Holden Village, possibly outnumbering the Lutherans, is bears. At night hang food and toilet articles and anything with an interesting odor, shape, or color from the cables provided at Revel Camp, Hart Lake, and Lower Lyman Lake. Elsewhere, stand by to bang pots. However, if you camp off the beaten track, in a spot the bears don't expect to find goodies,

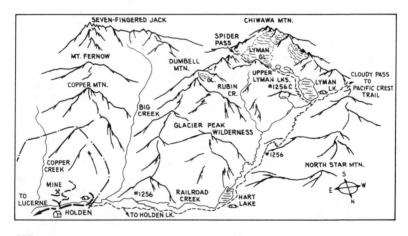

you may sleep in peace. If you choose a crowded camp on the principle of safety in numbers, your best chance of fun will be to have a large supply of flash bulbs and spend the night taking candid photos of half-dressed campers banging pots.

At ¾ mile from the road-end campground pass the Holden Lake trail. At 3½ miles skirt Hart Lake (camp), at 4½ miles Revel Camp (good sites), and at 7 miles reach the outlet of Lower Lyman Lake, 5587 feet (camps here and at the head of the lake).

The best is yet to come. Cross the outlet on trail No. 1256C and switchback up 500 feet, from subalpine forest and parkland into wide-open meadows. Pass the several Upper Lyman Lakes and at 10 miles from Holden come to the toe of the Lyman Glacier, 6000 feet.

The glacier has retreated from its maximum of the "Little Ice Age," as photographed by Professor Lyman, but still flows impressively from Chiwawa Mountain, 8459 feet, and is among the safest opportunities for a hiker to touch a living glacier.

The heather meadows near the middle of the Upper Lakes cannot withstand the impact of camping; set up housekeeping on the moraine near the glacier or on any bare soil 200 feet from water. Carry a stove; the wood here is too scarce and picturesque to waste in campfires.

Camping near the snout of the Lyman Glacier

99 AGNES CREEK—LYMAN LAKE LOOP

Loop trip 43 miles
Allow 3–7 days
High point 6438 feet
Elevation gain 4900 feet

Hikable mid-July through
  September
USGS McGregor Mountain, Mt.
  Lyall, Agnes Mountain,
  Stehekin, Holden

Here's a favorite of loopers: ascending one of the supreme long-and-wild, low-to-high valleys of the North Cascades to Suiattle Pass, then climbing over Cloudy Pass and descending past Lyman Lake and Holden Village to Lake Chelan.

Hikes from Lake Chelan involve unusual transportation to and from trailheads. In this case there are the *Lady of the Lake* (Hike 96), which drops the party off at Stehekin and picks it up at Lucerne, the Park Service shuttle bus up the Stehekin road, and the Lucerne bus down from Holden Village (Hike 98). The trip plan must take into account that hikers probably won't get started on the trail until midafternoon of the

Lyman Lake and Chiwawa Mountain from Cloudy Pass

first day and must be off the trail by midmorning of the last day to catch the boat.

From Stehekin Landing ride the bus 11 miles to High Bridge Ranger Station. About 500 feet beyond the bridge, on the left side of the road, is Agnes Creek trailhead (Pacific Crest Trail No. 2000), elevation 1600 feet.

The trail drops a few feet, crosses Agnes Creek, and commences a long, easy grade in lovely forest with notable groves of cedar. Glimpses ahead of Agnes Mountain and glaciers on Dome Peak; to the rear, McGregor Mountain. A good stop the first night is Fivemile Camp, 2300 feet.

Take an extra day here for a fine sidetrip (or, in early summer when the loop is too snowy, a destination). Cross the Agnes on a bridge and hike West Fork Agnes trail 3 miles to the dead-end at the edge of grassy Agnes Meadow, 2500 feet, beneath the high rock walls of Agnes Mountain and the glaciers of a half-dozen peaks. This sidetrip can be done in mid-June, when the meadow newly melted from the snow is all one yellow-and-white glow of glacier lily and spring beauty.

From Fivemile Camp the valley forest on the main trail continues superb, featuring a fine stand of large hemlock and fir near Swamp Creek; there's another good camp here at 8 miles.

At Hemlock Camp, 12 miles, the trail splits. The new Pacific Crest Trail crosses the river, climbs to high views on the side of the valley, and at 19 miles reaches timberline campsites at a junction, 5600 feet. You can also get here via the old valley trail, which may be the better choice in early summer, when the new trail is likely to be largely in snow.

For a mandatory sidetrip, go right at the junction 6 miles to Image Lake (Hike 12), for the day or overnight.

For the loop, go left over 6438-foot Cloudy Pass to Lyman Lake and another must-do sidetrip, to Upper Lyman Lake and Upper-Upper Lyman Lake, ringed by barren moraines left by the source of icebergs, the glacier flowing from 8459-foot Mt. Chiwawa (Hike 98).

Finish the loop down Railroad Creek to Holden Village, by bus to Lucerne, and boat down Lake Chelan.

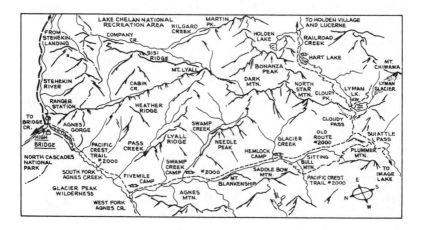

100   PACIFIC CREST TRAIL

One way from Stehekin River to
  Stevens Pass 98 miles
Allow 10–15 days
Elevation gain 17,000 feet
Hikable July through September

Some of the most pleasant flower-covered meadow country and spectacular scenery of the entire Pacific Crest Trail lie in this section, which traverses the side of Glacier Peak and walks the ridge tops south to Stevens Pass. One must make a choice of going east of Glacier Peak over famous Buck Creek Pass and spectacular Little Giant Pass, involving a hot and dusty 5-mile road walk, or going west of the peak through pleasant forest and alpine meadows.

Take the *Lady of the Lake* (Hike 96) to Stehekin and ride the Park Service shuttle bus up the Stehekin road to High Bridge Campground. Climb the Agnes valley to Suiattle Pass (Hike 99). Continue to Glacier Peak Mines (Hike 14) on the slopes of Plummer Mountain and choose either the east-of-Glacier or west-of-Glacier alternate.

East-of-Glacier alternate: Drop to Miners Creek, climb Middle Ridge, and continue to Buck Creek Pass (Hike 66). Descend Buck Creek to the old mining town of Trinity, walk the road to the Little Giant trail, cross Little Giant Pass (Hike 65) into the Napeequa valley, cross Boulder Pass (Hike 58) to the White River, and return via the White River trail to the Cascade Crest at Lower White Pass. **Distance from High Bridge to Lower White Pass 79 miles, elevation gain about 15,000 feet, hiking time 7 days.** The journey can be broken at either the Chiwawa River road or White River road.

West-of-Glacier alternate: Drop to the Suiattle River, climb the Vista Creek trail over ridges and down into Milk Creek (Hike 11), cross Fire Creek Pass to the White Chuck River (Hike 19), ascend the White Chuck to Red Pass, and continue via White Pass to Lower White Pass (Hike 57). **Distance from High Bridge to Lower White Pass 66 miles, elevation gain about 12,000 feet, hiking time 6 days.** The journey can be broken by trail exits to the Suiattle River road, White Chuck River road, or North Fork Sauk River road.

The remainder of the way to Stevens Pass is comparatively level, wandering along the Cascade Crest with ups and downs, frequently alternating from east side to west side, mostly through open meadows of flowers or heather. From Lower White Pass (Hike 57) the trail stays high, dipping into forest only at Indian Pass and again at Cady Pass. From Cady Pass the route contours hillsides, traversing a mixture of forest and meadows past Pear Lake (Hike 41), climbing within a few hundred feet of Grizzly Peak, and proceeding onward to Lake Janus (Hike 44), Union Gap, Lake Valhalla (Hike 43), and finally Stevens Pass. **Distance from Lower White Pass to Stevens Pass 32 miles, elevation gain 5000 feet, hiking time 4 days.**

Pacific Crest Trail on side of Indian Head Peak

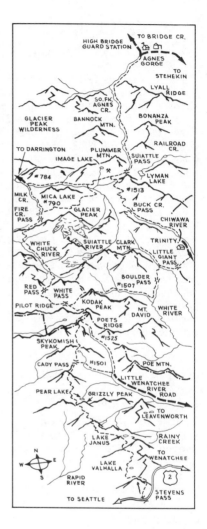

STILL MORE HIKES IN THE
GLACIER PEAK NORTH CASCADES

This volume, named after the highest mountain in the area, covers the 75 miles from the western foothills of the Cascade Mountains to the shores of Lake Chelan, and from Stevens Pass 50 miles north to Cascade Pass. The companion volumes are, *50 Hikes in Mount Rainier National Park, 100 Hikes in the Alpine Lakes, 100 Hikes in the South Cascades and Olympics,* and *100 Hikes in the North Cascades,* which, as the name implies, reaches to the Canadian border. Another, *103 Hikes in Southwestern British Columbia,* follows the Far North Cascades over the border to their end and extends into neighboring ranges. Shorter walks than those herein are described in *Trips and Trails 1: Family Camps, Short Hikes, and View Roads around the North Cascades.* The interface of lowlands and front ridges of the Cascades is treated in *Footsore 2 and 3: Walks and Hikes Around Puget Sound.* Approaches to and routes up peaks are the subject of *Cascade Alpine Guide,* a series of three volumes.

The 100 hikes have been selected to be representative of all the varied provinces of the Glacier Peak region. However, it's a big country with many other comparable trips. The books noted above describe many. Following is a sampling—some covered by the books, some not—that can be particularly recommended. The lack of detailed directions may be compensated for by greater solitude.

CASCADE RIVER
Kindy Creek: Little-used trail in a magnificent forest providing access to Kindy Creek.

SUIATTLE RIVER
Suiattle Mountain: From road No. 2640, 1 mile of unmaintained trail to Lake Tupso and White Creek road.
Canyon Lake and Totem Pass: A flower-covered ridge 5 miles from Image Lake.
Suiattle River to Suiattle Glacier: Magnificent forests. Trail is lost beyond Chocolate Creek. From there the route is for the experienced climber only.

WHITE CHUCK RIVER
Glacier Ridge: Shortcut to Pumice Cirque on a steep trail, partially maintained by a Boy Scout troop, past an old lookout site. Crystal Lake: 1½ miles to a lake in a deep valley.

SOUTH FORK STILLAGUAMISH RIVER
Heather Lake: Very popular 2-mile hike to alpine lake (*Footsore 3*).
Lake 22: Very popular 2½-mile hike to alpine lake (*Footsore 3*).
Pinnacle Lake: 1½ miles of poor trail to beautiful lake with views (*Footsore 3*).
Meadow Mountain: Tiny meadows on wooded ridge from Tupso Lake.
Silver Gulch trail: 1½ miles on old miners' path to open ridges.

SOUTH FORK SAUK RIVER

76 Gulch: An unmaintained route to old mines.

SKYKOMISH RIVER

Mt. Stickney: A route on logging roads and through bushes to high views (*Footsore 2*).

Mineral City-Silver Creek: Rich in mining history. The walk follows abandoned logging roads (*Footsore 2*).

Howard Creek: No trail, a bushwhacking climbers' route to Spire Mountain.

Troublesome Creek: Dead-end trail through the woods (*Trips and Trails 1*).

WENATCHEE RIVER

South Shore Wenatchee: Trail is a pleasant lakeshore path.

LITTLE WENATCHEE RIVER

Cockeye Creek trail: Over Poet Ridge to Panther Creek. Easy access to Poe Mountain from road No. 6504.

WHITE RIVER

Twin Lakes: Easy hike to popular mountain lakes.

Sears Creek: Unmaintained trail on Wenatchee Ridge.

Canyon Creek: Unmaintained trail on Wenatchee Ridge.

CHIWAWA RIVER

Leroy Creek: Steep trail to meadows and camps in a basin on the side of Mt. Maude, with access over the ridge to Ice Lakes.

Phelps Ridge: A trail going from Red Mountain trail over the ridge and down to Phelps Creek trail at a point just above Leroy Creek.

Massie Lake: 6-mile trail from Chiwawa Basin up to Massie Lake and then climbing under Pass No Pass to join the Buck Creek trail.

ENTIAT RIVER

Hornet Ridge: Trail goes 6 miles to alpine meadow.

Hardy Drive One: Abandoned trail goes 5 miles to alpine meadow.

Hardy Drive Two: Abandoned trail goes 5 miles to alpine meadow.

Billy Creek: Trail goes 5 miles to Tyee Ridge trail.

South Tommy: Trail goes 6 miles to Tyee Ridge trail.

Three Creek: Abandoned trail goes 4 miles to Entiat Range.

LAKE CHELAN-STEHEKIN RIVER

Holden Lake: 4-mile sidetrip from Railroad Creek to a lake in a hanging valley. Views of Mary Green Glacier on Bonanza Peak.

Flat Creek: Dead-end, 3⅓-mile trail into scenic valley under the LeConte Glacier.

Devore Creek-Company Creek loop: A long valley hike with a few meadows.

INDEX

Agnes Creek—230
Alder Creek—170
Alpine Baldy—112
Alpine Lookout—118, 126
Angle Peak—206
Ashland Lakes—91
Bachelor Meadows—46
Bald Eagle Mountain—73
Bald Mountain—90
Barclay Lake—106
Basalt Peak —150
Basalt Ridge—148, 198
Bedal Basin—76
Blanca Lake—102
Blue Creek Campground—172, 175, 178, 181, 182, 184
Blue Lake, Upper—73
Boiling Springs—186
Boulder Lake—101
Boulder Pass—55, 144, 159
Boulder River—34
Boulder River Wilderness—34, 37, 38, 86
Buck Creek Pass—55, 160
Byrne, Lake—64, 69
Cady Pass—105, 132
Camp Lake—65, 69
Carne Mountain—155, 157, 166
Cascade River
    Middle Fork—28
    South Fork—28
Circle Peak—40
Cloudy Pass—52, 231
Cougar Mountain—176, 182
Cow Creek—197, 201
Crow Hill—211, 222
Curry Gap—73
Cutthroat Lakes—91
David, Mount—138
Devils Backbone—208
Diamond Lake—61
Dickerman, Mount—96
Dirty Face Peak—136
Dishpan Gap—73, 103
Dolly Creek—49
Domke Lake—224

Downey Creek—46
Duncan Hill—192
Eagle Lake—106
Elliott Creek—78
Emerald Lake—61
Emerald Park—226
Entiat Meadows—202
Entiat Mountains View—184
Entiat River—182, 194, 200
    North Fork—212, 215, 216, 221, 223
Estes Butte—155, 156, 166
Fern Lake—216
Fifth of July Mountain—201
Finney Peak—31
Fire Creek Pass—57, 61, 63
Foggy (Crater) Lake—81
Fortune Ponds—110
Fourmile Ridge—208
Garland Peak (trail)—148, 197
Gee Point—31
Glacier Basin—84
Glacier Peak, Around—54
Glacier Peak Meadows—66
Glacier Peak Wilderness—28, 44, 46, 49, 54, 60, 62, 64, 66, 68, 138, 140, 142, 144, 158, 160, 162, 164, 200, 202, 226, 228, 230, 232
Glasses Lake—131
Goat Flats—86
Goat Lake—78
Gothic Basin—80
Green Mountain—44
Greider Lakes—100
Grizzly Peak—116
Hart Lake—228
Headlee Pass—98
Heather Lake—131
Hi Yu Trail—175
Higgins, Mount—32
High Bridge Ranger Station—231, 232
High Pass—160
Holden Village—53, 228, 230
Huckleberry Mountain—42

Ibex Creek—140
Ice Lakes—200, 202
Image Lake—50, 52, 55, 231
Indian Creek—142
Indian Head Peak—132, 142
Indigo Lake—40
Itswoot Lake—46
Jackson, Henry M., Wilderness—
  70, 72, 76, 78, 82, 84, 102, 104,
  110, 114, 116, 128, 131, 132
Janus, Lake—116
Joan Lake—109
Kelly Creek—112
Kennedy Hot Springs—62, 65,
  66, 69
Kennedy Ridge—62
Klone Peak—180, 188, 190
Kodak Peak—132
Lady Camp Basin—51
Lake Creek—206
Larch Lakes—200
Little Giant Pass—55, 158
Lone Tree Pass—37
Lost Creek Ridge—68
Lost Lake—177
Lyman Lake—52, 228, 230
  Upper—229, 231
Mad Lake—170, 172, 184
Mad River—170, 172, 175, 176,
  181, 184, 188
Mallardy Ridge—92
Marble Gulch—93
Marten Creek—92
Massie Lake—162
Meadow Mountain—60
Meander Meadows—132
Merritt Lake—118, 124
Milham Pass—202, 226
Milk Creek—49
Miners Ridge (Chiwawa)—168
Miners Ridge (Suiattle)—50, 52
Minotaur Lake—128
Monte Cristo—82, 84
Myrtle Lake—194, 197, 202
Napeequa Valley—55, 144, 158
Nason Ridge—118, 120, 122, 124,
  126
Neiderprum Trail—37
North Crest Cutoff Trail—113

North Tommy Ridge—181, 188
Pacific Crest National Scenic
  Trail—49, 53, 55, 105, 114,
  116, 132, 142, 232
Panther Creek—140
Peach Lake—110
Pear Lake—110
Peek-A-Boo Lake—58
Perry Creek—94
Pilchuck, Mount—89
Pilot Ridge—73
Poe Mountain—134
Pugh Ridge—214
Pyramid Creek, South—218, 220,
  223
Pyramid Mountain—211, 218
Raging Creek—146
Railroad Creek—52, 228, 231
Ray's Knoll—85
Red Mountain (trail)—162
Red Pass—66, 132, 142
Rock Creek—154, 166
Rock Lake—118, 122
Rock Mountain—118, 120, 122
Round Lake—69
Round Mountain—30
Saddle Lake—87
Sally Ann, Lake—105, 132
Schaefer Lake—153
Scorpion Mountain—109
Shetipo Creek—197, 198
Signal Peak—187
Silver Lake—82
Skykomish River, North Fork—
  105
Sloan Peak Meadows—70
Snowy Creek—119, 120
Spaulding Mine (trail)—28
Spider Glacier—165
Spider Meadow—162, 164
Squire Creek Pass—38
Stujack Pass—74
Suiattle Pass—51, 231
Suiattle River—49, 50, 52
Sunrise Mine (trail)—98
Three Fingers—87
Top Lake—111
Twin Lakes—82
Two Little Lakes—178, 181

Tyee Ridge—186
Union Gap—115, 116
Valhalla, Lake—114
Vista Creek—49
Wards Pass—105
West Cady Ridge—104

Whistling Pig Meadow—182
White Chuck Glacier—66
White Chuck River—57, 61, 65
White Pass—57
White River—55, 132, 142, 144